CAMDEN MARKET 4

Arbeitsheft Inklusion

Erarbeitet von
Gisela Ehlers und Christina Röwe

unter Mitwirkung der Redaktion
Britta Daugsch und Annika Meinhardt

**Herausgeber der bisherigen Reihe
und Berater der Programmleitung:**
Otfried Börner, StD a.D.,
Dr. phil. h.c. Christoph Edelhoff, StD a.D.

Diesterweg
westermann

CAMDEN MARKET 4

Materialien für Schülerinnen und Schüler
- Workbook 4 mit Lernsoftware und Audio-CD
  (ISBN 978-3-425-**73834**-5)
- Workbook 4 mit Audio-CD (ISBN 978-3-425-**73824**-6)
- Lernsoftware 4
  – Einzelplatzlizenz (ISBN 978-3-425-**73884**-0)
  – Schullizenz (ISBN 978-3-425-**73894**-9)
- Arbeitsheft Inklusion 4 mit Audio-CD
  (ISBN 978-3-425-**73784**-3)
- Kit 4 (ISBN 978-3-425-**73844**-4)
- Vocab-App 4 – kostenfreier Download unter
  https://play.google.com/store, Stichwort: „Diesterweg"

Materialien für Lehrkräfte
- Lehrerfassung zum Textbook 4 (ISBN 978-3-425-**73984**-7)
- Workbook 4 mit Lösungen und Audio-CD
  (ISBN 978-3-425-**73814**-7)
- Teacher's Manual mit Lösungen 4 (ISBN 978-3-425-**73864**-2)
- Vorschläge für Lernerfolgskontrollen 4
  (ISBN 978-3-425-**73914**-4)
- Audio-CD + DVD 4 für Lehrkräfte (ISBN 978-3-425-**73854**-3)
- Interaktive Whiteboard-Software 4
  – Einzelplatzlizenz (ISBN 978-3-425-**73934**-2)
  – Schullizenz (ISBN 978-3-425-**73994**-6)
- Folien 4 (ISBN 978-3-425-**73924**-1)
- Differenzierende Kopiervorlagen 4 (ISBN 978-3-425-**73874**-1)
- Differenzierende Kopiervorlagen für offenen Unterricht 4
  (ISBN 978-3-425-**73954**-0)

Vorbereiten. Organisieren. Durchführen.
BiBox ist das umfassende Digitalpaket zu diesem Lehrwerk
mit zahlreichen Materialien und dem digitalen Schulbuch.
Für Lehrkräfte und für Schülerinnen und Schüler sind verschiedene Lizenzen verfügbar. Nähere Informationen unter
www.bibox.schule

westermann GRUPPE

© 2016 Bildungshaus Schulbuchverlage Westermann Schroedel Diesterweg Schöningh Winklers GmbH,
Georg-Westermann-Allee 66, 38104 Braunschweig
www.westermann.de

Druck A³ / Jahr 2022
Alle Drucke der Serie A sind im Unterricht parallel verwendbar.

Redaktion: Britta Daugsch und Annika Meinhardt
Layout: Druckreif! Sandra Grünberg, Braunschweig
Illustrationen: Ulf Marckwort, Kassel
Umschlaggestaltung: blum design und kommunikation, Hamburg
Druck und Bindung: Westermann Druck GmbH, Georg-Westermann-Allee 66, 38104 Braunschweig

ISBN 978-3-425-73784-3

Welcome to the USA!

Liebe Schülerinnen und Schüler,

das *Camden Market Arbeitsheft Inklusion 4* lädt euch in diesem Schuljahr ein, die USA kennenzulernen. Ihr werdet eine Menge über die Menschen, die Sprache und die Kultur erfahren. Daher wird euch in einigen Hör- und Lesetexten *American English* begegnen.

Außerdem lernt ihr berühmte amerikanische Städte, Sehenswürdigkeiten und die Landschaften kennen.

Viel Spaß auf eurer Entdeckungsreise durch die USA!

Camden Market Arbeitsheft Inklusion 4

Mit diesem Rätsel kannst du den vierten Band vom Arbeitsheft Inklusion
kennen lernen und dein Wissen über die USA testen.
Dazu musst du ein bisschen blättern.
Vor jeder Antwortmöglichkeit steht ein Buchstabe.
Kreise immer den richtigen Buchstaben ein.
Du erhältst dann einen Lösungssatz.

1 Auf Seite 7 findest du das
Inhaltsverzeichnis.
Welches *Theme* beginnt auf Seite 23?
(W)   Let's grab some food.
(S)   What's up?

2 Auf Seite 58 begegnen dir
Native Americans.
Wer sind sie?
(E)   Amerikanische
        Ureinwohner.
(R)   Australische
        Ureinwohner.

3 Auf Seite 37 findest du eine Seite
aus einem New-York-Reiseführer.
**Welche Sehenswürdigkeit wird
rechts oben beschrieben?**
(O)   Times Square.
(C)   Central Park.

4 Auf Seite 8 werden bestimmte
Zeichen erklärt.
Was bedeutet dieses Zeichen?
(O)   Hier erfährst du interessante Dinge
        über die USA.
(S)   Hier erfährst du interessante Dinge
        über Großbritannien.

5 Auf Seite 83 werden Yosemite und
Death Valley genannt.
Was sind diese beiden?
(A)   Brücken.
(M)   Nationalparks.

Falls du nicht alles lösen kannst, versuche es am Ende des Schuljahres noch einmal.

6 Welche Farben hat die US-amerikanische Flagge?

(T)   Rot, weiß, grün.

(E)   Rot, weiß, blau.

7 Welcher Feiertag wird von vielen Amerikanern im November gefeiert?

(T)   Thanksgiving.

(R)   Halloween.

8 Womit bezahlen Amerikaner?

(O)   US Dollar ($).

(H)   Pfund Sterling (£).

9 Wofür steht die Abkürzung „USA"?

(O)   United Stars of America.

(U)   United States of America.

10 Wie viele Bundesstaaten haben die USA?

(D)   45 Bundesstaaten.

(S)   50 Bundesstaaten.

11 Was ist die Hauptstadt der USA?

(A)   Washington D.C.

(L)   New York City.

| _ | _ | L | _ | _ | _ | _ | _ | _ | | T | H | E | _ | _ | _ | ! |
|1|2| |3|4|5|6| |7|8| | | | |9|10|11|

Hast du das Rätsel gelöst? Super!

Viel Spaß im neuen Schuljahr!

Spielregeln

1. Ein Spieler würfelt und setzt seine Spielfigur auf das entsprechende Spielfeld. Ist es ein Spielfeld mit einem Text darauf, liest der Spieler den Text laut vor.
2. Wenn ein Spieler auf ein Feld mit einer Leiter kommt: Der Spieler darf seine Spielfigur die Leiter „hochklettern" lassen, um auf das Feld am Ende der Leiter vorzurücken.
3. Wenn ein Spieler auf ein Feld mit einer Schlange kommt: Der Spieler muss der Schlange folgen und auf das Feld zurückgehen, auf dem die Schlange endet.
4. Wer das Ziel zuerst erreicht, gewinnt.

start

30

29 Fortune cookies are from the USA, not China.

28

27

26

25 The Statue of Liberty has shoe size 876.

24

23

22

21

1

2

3

20 The first cheerleaders were men, not women.

19

18

17

16

15 Most pencils in the USA are yellow.

14

13

12

4 Most people in the USA speak English or Spanish.

5

6

7

8

9 The first man on the moon was American (Neil Armstrong).

10

11

Inhalt

Symbole und Verweise

Diese Dinge übst du:

 Hören

 Sprechen

 Wortschatz

 Lesen

 Schreiben

 Hier kannst du auf Deutsch z. B. über englische Schilder sprechen.

 Dieser Text ist auf CD. Die Zahl in der CD nennt die CD-Nummer.
Die Zahl unter der CD gibt die Tracknummer an.

 Diese Aufgabe ist ein bisschen schwieriger.

 Hier gibt es eine thematisch passende Aufgabe im
Camden Market Textbook.
Die obere Zahl nennt die Aufgabennummer,
die untere die Seitenzahl.

Wörter in grauer Schrift kannst du in deinen eigenen Sätzen
austauschen.

Diese Kästen werden dir im Buch begegnen:

 Hier erfährst du interessante Dinge über die USA.

 Hier findest du wichtige Redemittel.

 Hier findest du Tipps zum Englischlernen.

 Hier bekommst du Tipps zu den Aufgaben.

Theme 1

Hi to high school!

In diesem *Theme* ...

- beschäftigst du dich mit amerikanischen Schulen und ihren Besonderheiten.
- lernst du Unterschiede zwischen britischem und amerikanischem Englisch kennen.
- bereitest du eine Kurzpräsentation über deinen Schulalltag vor.
- beschäftigst du dich mit dem Thema Recycling.
- sprichst du darüber, was du für die Umwelt tun kannst.

1

1 Guess

 p. 18/19

Look at the photos.
Guess what the things are.

I think the first photo is a …

1

2

3

2 School words

 p. 18/19

a) Circle the words in the correct colour:

Zwei Wörter bleiben übrig.

subjects    things in schoolbags   school clubs

English	cafeteria	folder	art
sports club	history	lockers	exercise book
computer club	ruler	drama club	

b) Look at the photos.
Then write down the words.

Die Wörter findest du
im Kasten bei a).

1

2

_____   _____

c) Listen and check.

3 American school life

1
p. 18/19

2

a) Listen and number (1–4).

_____

_____

_____

_____

b) Complete the words.
Then write them under the photos in a).

oo • ee • ff • oo • ll

ch___ ___rleaders   American f___ ___tba___ ___

sch___ ___l bus   security o___ ___icer

1
3

c) Listen and check.

4 American high schools

a) Read the sentences. Complete them.

Die Aufgaben 2 und 3 helfen dir.

1. Many high schools have s___ ___ _u_ ___ ___ ___y officers.

2. The s___ ___ ___ ___ ___ bus is always yellow.

3. Pupils put their books into l___ ___ ___ ___ _r_ ___.

4. C___ ___ ___ _r_ _l_ ___ ___ _d_ ___ ___ ___ dance and sing

   at sports events.

5. Pupils eat their lunch in the c___ _f_ ___ ___ ___ ___ ___a.

b) Talk to your partner. What is different to your school?

We don't have security officers at our school.

...

We have ..., too.

Land und Leute

Im Vergleich zu amerikanischen Highschools werden dir einige Unterschiede zu deutschen Schulen auffallen. Alle Lehrer haben ihren eigenen Raum. Die Schüler müssen zu ihnen kommen. Jeder Schüler besitzt einen Schülerausweis (*ID card*) mit Foto, den er immer bei sich tragen muss. Außerdem bekommen amerikanische Schüler Buchstaben als Noten: A, B, C, D und F, also keine Zahlen. Es gibt Schulfächer, die alle Schüler belegen müssen, und ein Kursangebot mit Wahlfächern (*electives*).

Wie ist es bei dir an der Schule?

5 Gillian's first day at Lake Park High School

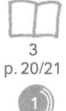

3
p. 20/21

1

4

a) **Listen. What did you understand?**

 USA.

School.

Timetable.

Ihr könnt die Wörter
an der Tafel sammeln.

b) **Listen again and read along.**
Then colour the words from a) in the dialogue.

Gillian is visiting Cheryl and her family in the USA.
Today is Cheryl's first day of school after her summer vacation.

Gillian: So, what's your timetable for today?

Cheryl: My timetable?
Oh, you mean my class schedule.

Gillian: Yes. What lessons do you have?

Cheryl: I've got English, math, science and geography.
And after lunch I have American history and web design.
Web design is my elective.

Gillian: Your what?

Cheryl: It's my elective.
Students choose it from different subjects.

Gillian: Students? Oh, you mean pupils! That's funny!

c) **Underline the American words in the dialogue.**
Then complete the table.

British English	American English
summer holidays	
timetable	
pupils	

6 British or American?

a) Listen and tick. Is it British English or American English?

	British	American
1. "Let's go to the cinema and watch 'Batman'."		
2. "Excuse me, where are the <u>restrooms</u>?"		
3. "Come on! Let's take the subway!"		
4. "Would you like fries with your cheeseburger?"		
5. "There's a great football match on TV on Tuesday. Let's watch it."		
6. "I want to buy some new CDs. Let's go to the shopping centre."		
7. "I'm going on vacation in August."		

b) Underline the American words. un

c) Look at a) again. Complete the table.

British English 🇬🇧	American English 🇺🇸
toilets	*restrooms*
chips	
underground	*subway*
holiday	
cinema	the movies
	shopping mall
	soccer

7 What to do?

a) Read the website. Circle the electives.

5 p.22
6 p.23

Lake Park High School
Education is everything!

Here is a list of our electives.
If you have questions or need help,
please email Mr. Samuel.

- keyboarding
- Spanish
- photography
- drama
- video game design
- wood working class
- web design

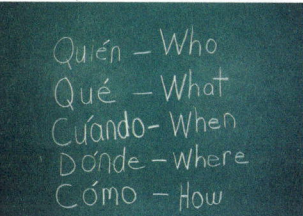

b) Listen and tick.

1. Andy wants to choose   a room   an elective.

2. Andy doesn't like   keyboarding   drama.

3. Andy's best friend speaks   Italian   Spanish.

4. Andy will take   photography   Spanish.

 c) Look at a) again. Then talk to your partner.
What would you choose?

I'd choose photography.
And you?

I'd choose …

8 **Your school**

7
p. 23

Make a word web about <u>your</u> school life.

teachers:

_____

_____

_____

subjects:

_____

_____

_____

_____:

_____

_____

my
school life

_____:

_____

_____

school clubs:

_____

_____

_____

cafeteria:

_____

_____

_____

Wenn du etwas präsentieren möchtest, ist es gut, wenn du deine Klasse
zu Beginn begrüßt und dann das Thema nennst.
Du solltest möglichst ruhig, deutlich und frei sprechen. Ablesen klingt oft
langweilig. Vergiss nicht, zwischendurch auch mal auf dein Poster zu
zeigen. Zum Schluss bedankst du dich für die Aufmerksamkeit der Zuhörer.
Falls du vorher etwas Zeit hast und du dich besonders gut vorbereiten
möchtest, kannst du deinen Vortrag mehrmals üben.
Präsentiere dein Poster z.B. deinen Eltern oder Geschwistern.

9 **Your school life**

7
p. 23

a) **Make a poster about <u>your</u> school life.**

Du kannst auch malen oder Fotos aufkleben. Ideen findest du bei Aufgabe 8.

My school life

b) **Present your poster in class.**

10 Acting green at school

a) Look at the picture. What can you see?

8
p. 24

There's ... / There are ...   I can see a bin.

b) Listen and number (1–4).   Zwei Szenen bleiben übrig.

1
7

c) Match the sentences and the people.

Some people don't turn off the lights.

A boy goes to school by car.

A girl leaves rubbish behind.

A boy doesn't recycle his plastic bottle.

11 Things you can do

9/10
p. 25

a) **Make a flyer.**
How can you help nature?

Du kannst auch ein Wörterbuch benutzen.

> **turn off the lights when you leave the room** •
> **sort your rubbish** • **go to school by bike** •
> **plant your own school garden** • ...

Let's help nature!

You can ...

b) **Present your flyer in class.**

1

12 Cleaning up

**a) Listen.
What is it about?**

12 p.26

8

b) Listen again. Underline the correct words.

1. Joel finds old baseball / basketball magazines in his locker.

2. Gary wants to keep / throw away the magazines.

3. The old magazines go into the paper / plastic container.

4. Gary doesn't know what to do with the full / empty milk bottles.

5. He finds a jacket / T-shirt on his locker.

13 Recycling

a) Circle the rubbish: plastic   paper   glass

12 p.26

 magazine

 old newspaper

glass bottle

 plastic bag

yoghurt cup

 old poster

b) Check with your partner.

Where would you put the newspaper?

I'd put it in the paper container.

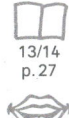

14 Take action!

13/14
p. 27

Play the game.

1. Form a group of three.
   Then look at the pictures A–E.

2. One of you chooses a picture and mimes the activity.

3. The other two have to guess the activity.

4. The one who says the correct activity first wins.

Plant a tree!

Sort rubbish!

Save energy!

That's right!

A
"save water"

B
"plant a tree"

C
"sort rubbish"

D
"go by bike"

E
"save energy"

Complete the wordbank.

Wörter, die du mit amerikanischen
Highschools verbindest:

(→ Seite 10 – 12)

– *security officer*

_____

_____

_____

Wahlfächer an einer Highschool:

(→ Seite 15)

– *keyboarding*

_____

_____

_____

Wörter, die du mit dem Thema Umweltschutz
verbindest:

(→ Seite 20, 21)

– *sort rubbish*

_____

_____

_____

Dieses Wort fandest du am einfachsten:

_____

Theme 2

Let's grab some food

In diesem *Theme* …

- beschäftigst du dich mit Lebensmitteln.
- erfährst du etwas über Essgewohnheiten in den USA.
- beschäftigst du dich mit Fastfood.
- lernst du, einen Feedbackbogen auf Englisch auszufüllen.
- lernst du verschiedene Feste und Bräuche in den USA kennen.

1 Are you hungry?

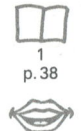

1
p. 38

a) Look at the picture.
Then talk to your partner.
How many food and drink words
do you know?

Du kannst auch weitere Lebensmittel zeichnen und nennen.

b) Write down the words from a).
Make two lists.

Du kannst auch ein
Wörterbuch benutzen.

Things you put in the fridge:

Things you put on the shelf:

c) Find more words. Write them down in the lists in b).

2 A lunch game

1
p. 38

Play the game with your partner.

Du findest das Spiel
bei Aufgabe I im Anhang.

1. Tell your partner what you
   have for lunch today.

2. Check with your partner.

> I've got a sausage, a salad,
> lemonade, a banana, …

> A salad, a banana, …

3 Funny English

1
p. 38

9–10

Listen and repeat.

For fine fresh fish, phone Phil!

Fred fed Ted bread.

1

2

2
p. 38/39

1
11–18

4 Typical American food?

a) Listen and number the photos.

I like peanut butter and jelly on bread.
That's my lunch!

Sam

Alaska

I love chicken, green beans
and mashed potatoes.
YUMMY!

Ezra

California

Arizona

Jerry

I love chili con carne!
I often cook it for friends.

1 **Jerry**

I often have burgers and fries.
I think that's typical American food.

Cody

Sieh dir vorher
die Karte an.

b) Listen again.
Then write the names in the correct box on the map.

Je

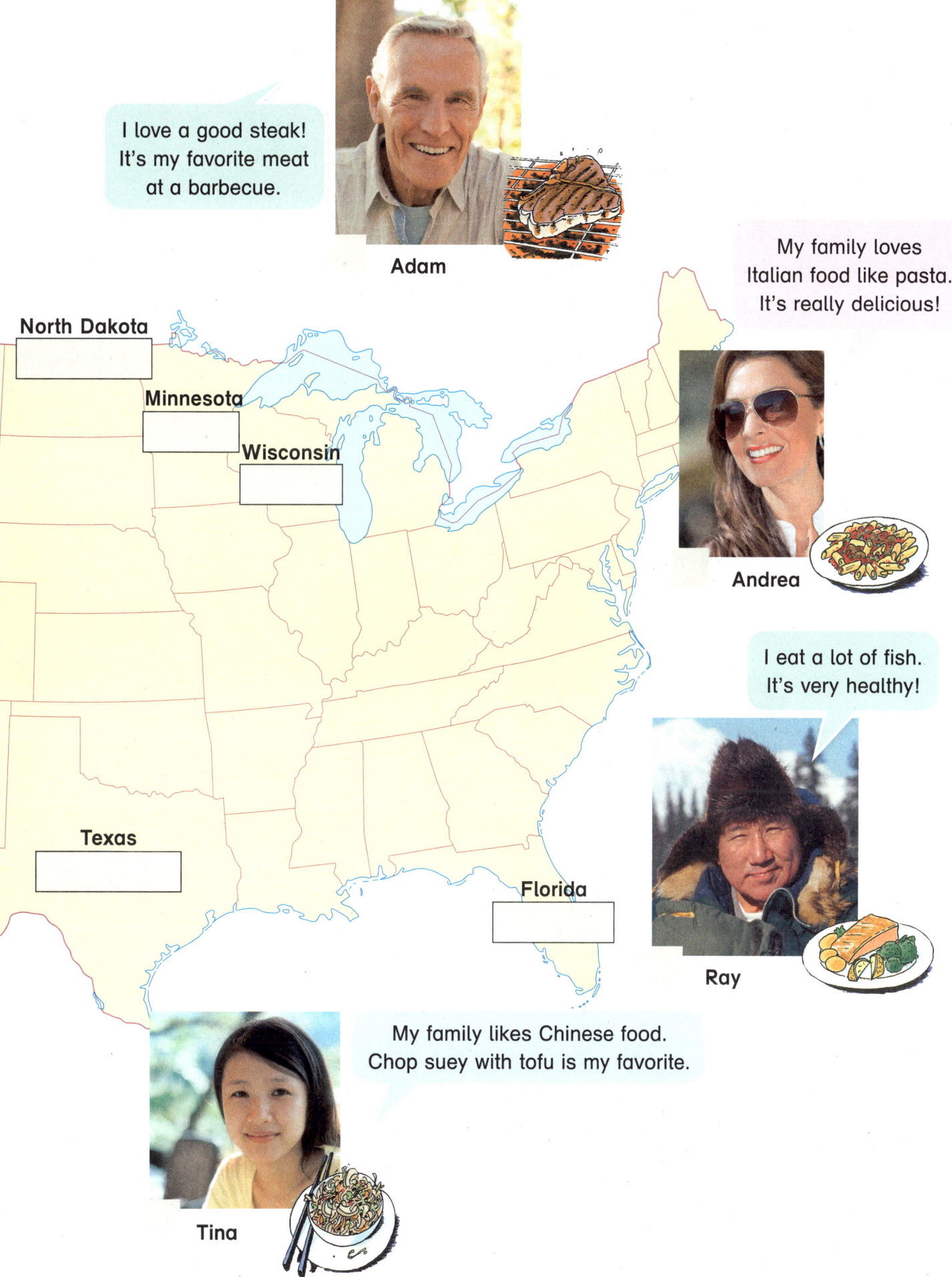

I love a good steak! It's my favorite meat at a barbecue.

Adam

My family loves Italian food like pasta. It's really delicious!

Andrea

North Dakota

Minnesota

Wisconsin

I eat a lot of fish. It's very healthy!

Ray

Texas

Florida

My family likes Chinese food. Chop suey with tofu is my favorite.

Tina

5 Have you ever tried …?

a) Listen and speak along.

3
p. 39
4
p. 40

19

Have you ever tried?	Yes, I have! Yes, I have!
Have you ever tried?	And I think …
Have you ever tried …	It's delicious!
a burger?	No! It's awful!

Have you ever tried?	No, I haven't! No, I haven't!
Have you ever tried?	But I think …
Have you ever tried …	It's great!
chili con carne?	No! It's disgusting!

b) Complete the sentences.

> Du kannst auch eigene Lebensmittel wählen.

1. *A hot dog is* _____ delicious.

2. _____ great.

3. _____ OK.

4. _____ awful.

5. _____ disgusting.

 c) Make your own chant. Present it in class.

6 Super Burger

Cheryl wants to write an article for the high school magazine.
She interviews Kathy.

6/7
p. 41

1
20

a) Listen to Cheryl's interview. What is it about?

   a burger restaurant   a steakhouse

b) Listen again.   7,000 • 12h every day • Roselle Deluxe •
Take notes.   6,000 • Roselle Special • 24h every day

When open?

How many burgers per day?

Which burgers most?

c) Complete Cheryl's article.

Great burgers – great place!

Last weekend I interviewed Kathy,
the manager of a cool burger restaurant.
It is a great place!

It is open _____ every day.

They sell over _____ per day.

They sell the _____ most.

7 A feedback form

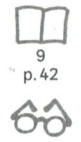

a) **Read the feedback form. What is it about?**

9
p.42

Joe's Corner
4560 Lincoln Road, Philadelphia, PA 19135

Takeaway:	✗ yes	○ no	
Food:	✗ delicious	○ OK	○ awful
Service:	○ friendly	✗ OK	○ unfriendly
Price:	○ cheap	✗ OK	○ expensive

What did you like?

✗ food   ○ service   ○ price

What didn't you like?

○ food   ✗ service   ○ price

What did you eat?

hamburger

Will you visit the restaurant again?

✗ yes   ○ no   ○ don't know

Other comments:

_____

Thank you for the feedback!

☐ a restaurant

☐ a shop

b) **Write down sentences.**

Schreibe ganze Sätze.

The name of the restaurant is _____.

It is in _____.

The food was _____.

_____

_____

_____

 c) **Compare with your partner.**

8 Your feedback form

9
p. 42

a) Fill in the feedback form for <u>your</u> favourite restaurant or <u>your</u> school cafeteria.

Name of the place: _____

Address: _____

_____

Takeaway: yes   no

Food: delicious   OK   awful

Service: friendly   OK   unfriendly

Price: cheap   OK   expensive

What did you like?

   food   service   price

What didn't you like?

   food   service   price

What did you eat?

_____

Will you visit the restaurant again?

   yes   no   don't know

Thank you for the feedback!

b) Present your restaurant in class. Look at 7b) for help.

I went to Star Pizza. It's in Kleiweg. …

9 Time to celebrate

a) Read the texts. Match the photos and the texts.

p. 44/45

1
On 17 March it is St Patrick's Day. It is an Irish holiday. There is a parade in New York City and other American cities. People wear green and eat green food.

2
In November, Americans celebrate Thanksgiving. Families and friends meet. Most of them have a special meal and eat turkey.

3
On 5 May Mexicans in the USA celebrate their culture. This day is called Cinco de Mayo.

4
Halloween is on 31 October. Children wear costumes and collect sweets. It is an Irish holiday but people in the USA celebrate it, too.

5
For Eid, Muslims meet with their families and friends. They have lots of special food and the children get sweets.

6
Most people in the USA celebrate Christmas on 25 December. Then they give presents to their families and friends.

b) Talk to your classmates. Do you celebrate any of these festivals?

In my family we celebrate Christmas.

We don't celebrate Cinco de Mayo.

We celebrate Eid.

10 Festivals in the USA

a) Read the blog entry.

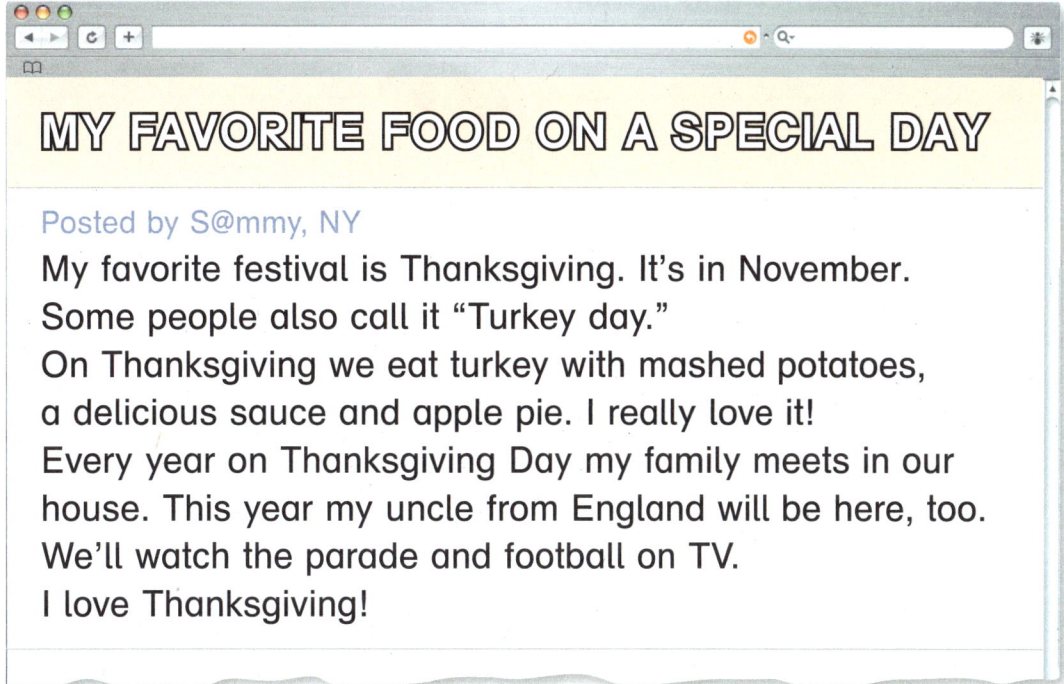

MY FAVORITE FOOD ON A SPECIAL DAY

Posted by S@mmy, NY

My favorite festival is Thanksgiving. It's in November.
Some people also call it "Turkey day."
On Thanksgiving we eat turkey with mashed potatoes,
a delicious sauce and apple pie. I really love it!
Every year on Thanksgiving Day my family meets in our
house. This year my uncle from England will be here, too.
We'll watch the parade and football on TV.
I love Thanksgiving!

b) Colour the food words and the activities in the text:

food words    activities

c) Write about your favourite festival.

My favourite festival is _____.

It is _____

_____

_____

_____

_____

_____

_____

Complete the wordbank.

Lebensmittel und Gerichte: (→ Seite 24–27)

– chili con carne _____

_____

_____

_____

Wörter, die beschreiben, wie etwas schmeckt: (→ Seite 28)

– delicious _____

_____

_____

_____

Feiertage, die in den USA gefeiert werden: (→ Seite 32)

– Halloween _____

_____

_____

_____

New places, new faces

3

In diesem *Theme* ...

- erfährst du Interessantes über Sehenswürdigkeiten in New York.
- lernst du verschiedene Stadtteile New Yorks kennen.
- planst du eine Tour durch Manhattan.
- beschäftigst du dich mit dem Alltag von Jugendlichen in anderen Teilen der Welt.
- liest du über *Fairtrade*.

1 New York City

a) Look at the photos.
What can you see?

1
p. 58

I can see a man.

There's …

There are …

21

b) Listen and number the photos (1–6).

c) Check with your partner.

2 Things to see in New York

2/3
p. 58/59

a) Read the information.

Die Informationen kannst du dir hier anhören: .

The Statue of Liberty

– is a symbol of freedom
– can be seen on a boat tour
– is 46 m high

Central Park

– is one of the biggest parks
  in New York
– is great for doing sports
– has a very big zoo

The Empire State Building

– has 102 floors
– has 1,860 steps
– is 443 m high

Times Square

– is in the heart of Manhattan
– is famous for its very big ads
– has many shops and restaurants

Chinatown

– is home to many
  Chinese people in New York
– has many Chinese restaurants
– celebrates Chinese New Year
  with a parade every year

Ground Zero

is where:
– the World Trade Center stood
– many people died
  on 11 September 2001
– there is now a memorial

b) Close your book. What do you remember?

There was Ground Zero.

3 Sights in the city

5
p. 60/61

**Look at the photos.
Choose one photo and describe it.**

Denke an *who*, *where* und *what*. Benutze auch ein Wörterbuch.

Chinatown

I can see people. There are ...

The Empire State Building at night on St Patrick's Day

View of One World Trade Center and Lower Manhattan

Grand Central Terminal

Brooklyn Bridge

The Rockefeller Center Christmas Tree

 **Land und Leute**

New York City, oder auch *The Big Apple*, ist mit über acht Millionen Einwohnern die größte Stadt in den USA. Es ist aber nicht die Hauptstadt. Das ist nämlich Washington D.C. Die Stadt New York hat fünf Stadtteile (*boroughs*): Manhattan, Brooklyn, die Bronx, Staten Island und Queens.

Was weißt du noch über New York?

4 Visit New York

7
p. 62

a) Put the pictures of the sights on the map.
Look at number 2 for help.

b) Check with your partner.

c) Glue the pictures onto the map.

> Denke daran, die Bilder
> erst in Teilaufgabe c)
> aufzukleben.
> Du findest sie bei
> Aufgabe II im Anhang.

dw_0011

N

Hudson River

Eleventh Avenue

West 23rd Street

Chelsea

West 14th Street

Greenwich Village

Avenue of the Americas

Westside Street

Canal Street

Lower West Side

Union Square

Liberty Island

The Statue of Liberty

Ground Zero

Broadway

Soho

Bowery

East 14th Street

Downtown

Battery Park

Wall Street

Chinatown

East Houston Street

East Village

Brooklyn Bridge

Lower East Side

Manhattan Bridge

Williamsburg Bridge

5 Your tour through Manhattan

a) Which tour would you take? Draw it on the map.

7
p. 62

First I'd visit Chinatown.
Then I'd go to the Empire State Building. …

b) Present your tour in class.

6 From Manhattan to the Bronx

a) Read the information about New York.

6
p. 62
8
p. 63

42

Visit
New York

In Manhattan you can see big skyscrapers. There are lots of famous sights.

Don't miss a baseball match at Yankee Stadium in the Bronx! You can also go for a nice walk in the zoo.

You can watch a tennis match in Queens. Or you can visit the Hall of Science.

You can walk across the Brooklyn Bridge to Brooklyn. There you can spend time at the amusement park.

Go to Staten Island by ferry: enjoy the beautiful beach.

b) Underline the five boroughs in the texts. un

7 Tourists in New York

a) Listen to the tourists and tick.

6
p.62
8
p.63

1
23

1. John is interested in ☐ skyscrapers ☐ bridges.

2. Sue and Mia want to ☐ visit a museum ☐ go to the beach.

3. Paul's hobby is ☐ basketball ☐ baseball.

b) Look at number 6 again.
Then write down tips for the tourists.
Use the words from the box.

> the Bronx • Manhattan • Staten Island •
> beach • baseball • skyscrapers

Where should the tourists go?

1. I think John should go to _____ because he

   is interested in _____.

2. I think Sue and Mia should go to _____

   because they want to _____.

3. I think Paul _____

   because his hobby _____.

c) Talk to your partner.

Where should John go?   I think John should go to …
                          because …

d) Listen and check.

1
24

8 Quiz time

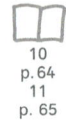

10
p. 64
11
p. 65

Work in groups.
Make a quiz about New York.
Look at number 2 for help.

> Die Quizkarten findest du
> bei Aufgabe III im Anhang.

1. Cut out the quiz cards.

2. Write questions on the blank cards.
   Use a dictionary.

3. Swap your cards with another group.
   Correct the mistakes.

4. Do the quiz in class.
   Ask your classmates or your teacher.

> Oft siehst du deine eigenen Fehler nicht. Manchmal hilft es, wenn ihr
> euch gegenseitig korrigiert. Damit deine Texte also richtig gut werden,
> solltest du sie mit Mitschülern tauschen. Dann könnt ihr eure Texte
> gegenseitig verbessern.

9 Different lives

13
p. 66
15
p. 67

25

a) **Listen and read along.**

Hi, my name is Allimar.
I am ten years old. I live with
my father, my sister and my two
brothers in Sri Lanka.
My father is a farmer.
He doesn't earn enough money.
So my mother went to Saudi
Arabia to find work.
Now I have to help a lot in the
house. I get up very early and
make a fire for tea. Then I make
breakfast for my family.
School starts at 9 o'clock.
When I get back home from
school I make lunch.
Then I clean the house.
In the evening I do my homework
and then I go to bed at half past nine.
I am often tired.

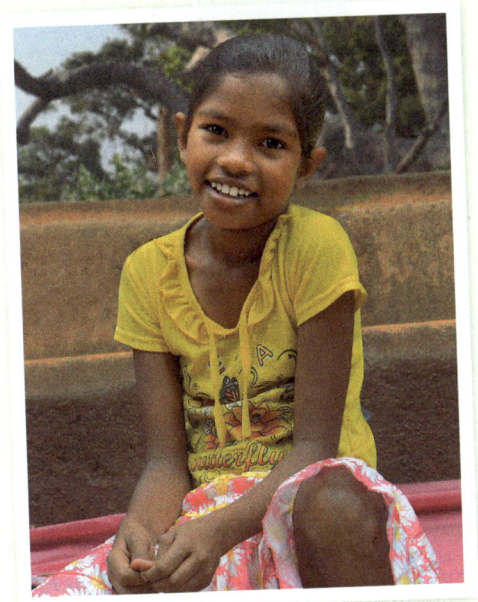

b) **Read again. Is it true or false?**   true   false

1. Allimar is from England.

2. She has got two sisters.

3. Her father is a farmer.

4. Her mother works in the USA.

5. Allimar doesn't help a lot in the house.

6. She doesn't go to school.

7. She is often tired.

10 Fairtrade

p. 68/69

a) Read the website.

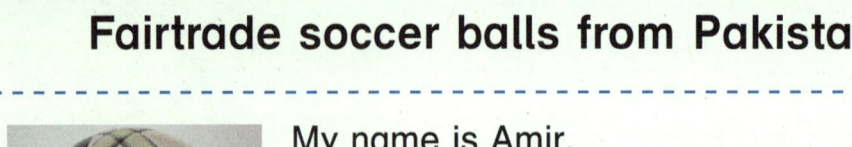

Fairtrade soccer balls from Pakistan

My name is Amir.
I am from Pakistan.
I work in a soccer ball factory.
I live in Pakistan with my family.

FAIRTRADE

Three years ago we were very poor.
My children couldn't go to school.
They had to work in the soccer ball factory,
too.

But then our lives changed.
We started to make Fairtrade
soccer balls.
Fairtrade is good. We have more
money now.

My children can go to school now.
They will have a better life later.

Fairtrade is also good for you:
Fairtrade soccer balls are cheaper than other soccer balls.
Fairtrade soccer balls only cost about $9.80.

Order your Fairtrade soccer ball now!

b) Read again. Circle the correct words.

1. Amir is from Pakistan / Afghanistan.

2. He works on a farm / in a factory.

3. His children couldn't go to school / were good at school.

4. His children / teachers had to work in the factory, too.

c) Read again. Complete the sentences.

1. They started to make _____

_____

2. Amir's children can _____

_____

3. Fairtrade balls are _____

_____

d) Compare with your partner.

Land und Leute

In ärmeren Ländern bekommen die meisten Landwirte keine fairen Preise für das, was sie herstellen. Sie können deshalb kaum ihre Familien ernähren. *Fairtrade* sorgt dafür, dass diese Menschen einen fairen Preis für ihre Produkte erhalten. Dies hilft ihnen dabei, ein besseres Leben zu führen: Die Familien können ihre Kinder zur Schule schicken und haben Geld für Medikamente. Jedes *Fairtrade*-Produkt hat eine Kennzeichnung.

Hast du den Begriff *Fairtrade* schon einmal gehört oder gelesen? Was hältst du von der Idee?

Complete the wordbank.

Sehenswürdigkeiten in New York: (→ Seite 37 – 42)

– *Central Park*

_____

_____

_____

_____

Diese Wörter verbindest du mit *Fairtrade*: (→ Seite 46, 47)

– *money* _____   _____

_____   _____

_____   _____

Dieses Wort fandest du am wichtigsten:

_____

Finding your place

In diesem *Theme* ...

- informierst du dich über Einwanderer in Amerika.
- erfährst du Eckdaten der amerikanischen Geschichte.
- lernst du die Familiengeschichte amerikanischer Teenager kennen.
- beschäftigst du dich mit der Bevölkerung der USA.
- erfährst du Interessantes über die Ureinwohner Amerikas.

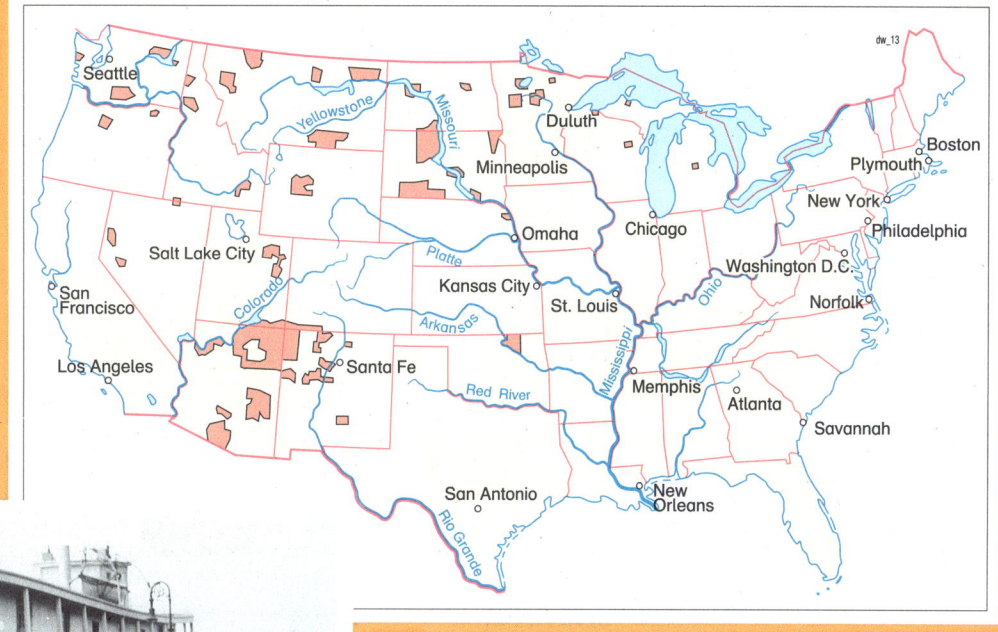

1 Tourists in America

1
p. 80/81

a) Look at the photos. What can you see?

I can see a boy with a red pullover.

There's …

There are …

b) Talk to your partner. Guess: Who is American?

I think the boy with the cap is American.

2
1

c) Listen. Then complete the sentence.

"We are __a__ ___ ___   __A__ ___ ___ ___ ___ __c__ ___ ___."

2 Many people, one nation

1
p.80/81

2
2

a) Listen and read along.

Many years ago, the first people came to America from Siberia. Now people call them "Native Americans". The Europeans came to America in 1492. Life was very hard for Native Americans. Many of them even died. Today many of them live on reservations.

A

B

In 1607 the first settlers came from England by ship. Then more and more people from Europe came. They hoped to find good farmland and freedom.

The settlers bought slaves from Africa to do the hard work for them. The first slaves arrived in 1619. Life was very hard for them. They had to fight for their rights.

C

D

In the 1860s a lot of Chinese people came to the USA. They worked on the railroad. Today many Chinese immigrants live in San Francisco.

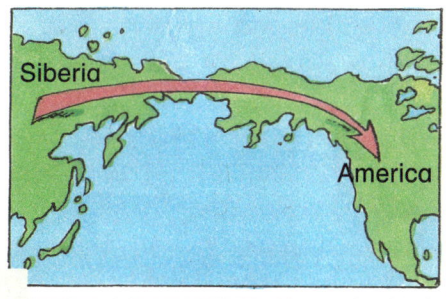
Siberia
America

 b) Match the pictures and the information.

c) Look at the texts again. Ask your partner.

Who worked on the railroad?

Who came from Siberia?

Who bought slaves from Africa?

3 Leaving home

Many people move to the USA every year.
Some people want to leave home.
Some people have to leave home.

3
p. 82

a) Complete the sentences.

food • work • money • love • war

1. "My parents can't find ___ ___ ___ ___.
   They hope to find jobs in the USA."

2. "We left home because there was ___ ___ ___.
   Life was very dangerous at home."

3. "My family is from a poor country.
   We left our home to earn more ___ ___ ___ ___ ___."

4. "There's not enough ___ ___ ___ ___ for our family where I
   come from. We moved to New York and we're not hungry now."

5. "Mum fell in ___ ___ ___ ___ with an American.
   We moved to the USA in May."

b) Check with your partner.

**c) Look at a) again.
Write down more ideas.**

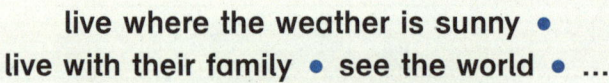
live where the weather is sunny •
live with their family • see the world • ...

People leave home because they want to ... _____

_____

_____

_____

4 Some facts about the USA

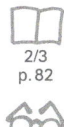

2/3
p. 82

a) Read the article.

53

Did you know that ...?

About 318 million people live in the USA today. That is more than 4% of the world's population. Some of these people come from all over the world.
But there are also about 12 million illegal immigrants in the USA. Many of them are from Mexico and South and Central America. But why did they leave their homes?

Lots of illegal immigrants came to the USA because they wanted a better life.
The USA is a very rich country and there are lots of jobs.

Immigrants from Mexico and South and Central America often only speak Spanish. That is why many signs are in English and Spanish.

Today it is not easy to immigrate to the USA. You need a "green card" to move to the USA. With a "green card" you can work and live there.

b) Colour the people in the article.

Ihr könnt Fragen an der Tafel oder auf einem Zettel sammeln.

c) Do a quiz in class. Ask 'who questions'. Look at 2 c) for help.

5 Family histories

a) Choose <u>one</u> person.
Then read about his / her life.

4
p. 83
5
p. 84

Die Texte kannst du dir
hier anhören: ②.
3–5

"Hi, I'm Mohamed. I'm 16 years old.
We left Somalia because of the war.
We lived on a farm in Somalia. Now we live
in a small apartment in New York.
My dad works very hard. My parents hope
that my sisters and I will be good at school.
They hope that we'll get good jobs later."

"Hi, I'm Kim. I'm from Vietnam. I'm
15 years old. My parents and I moved to
the USA. At first I couldn't speak English,
so I had a lot of problems. But the teachers
and the students helped me. I miss my old
friends from Vietnam. But everybody is nice
here and I have some new friends now."

"Hi, I'm Sergio. I'm 14 years old. My father
and I live in San Francisco now. Dad didn't
have a job in Chile. We came to the USA
for a better life. I couldn't speak English.
But my best friend Alek helped me a lot."

b) Underline important information about your person.
Find out about:

1. his / her name and age   un

2. where he / she is from   un

3. his / her problems   un

c) Complete the table for your person.

name	age	comes from	problem
			– there is war in Somalia
Kim			
		Chile	

d) Ask your classmates about the other persons.
   Complete the table in c).

What's Mohamed's problem?

How old is Sergio?

Where does Kim come from?

Wenn du erzählen möchtest, **was eine andere Person über
sich selbst gesagt hat**, musst du einige Wörter verändern:

I am …	–	**He / She is** …
My parents …	–	**His / Her** parents …
We lived …	–	**They** lived …
Our house …	–	**Their** house …
… for **me**.	–	… for **him / her**.

Statistiken sind nicht immer einfach zu lesen. Es gibt viele Zahlen, die neben- und übereinander stehen. Oft gibt es schwierige Prozentzahlen. Viele Wörter sind schwer verständlich. Da verliert man schnell den Überblick. Es gibt aber ein paar Tricks, die dir beim Lesen einer Statistik helfen.

– Überlege zuerst, was das Thema der Statistik ist. Überschriften helfen dir dabei.
– Oft werden Zahlen bildlich dargestellt, z.B. in Torten- oder Säulendiagrammen. Die Bilder zeigen dir die Verhältnisse an. So kannst du dir die Zahlen besser vorstellen.
– Du musst nicht jedes einzelne Wort verstehen. Oft genügt es, wenn du die wichtigsten Wörter verstehst.

6 People in the USA

Look at the statistics.
Then answer the questions in German.

2
p. 82

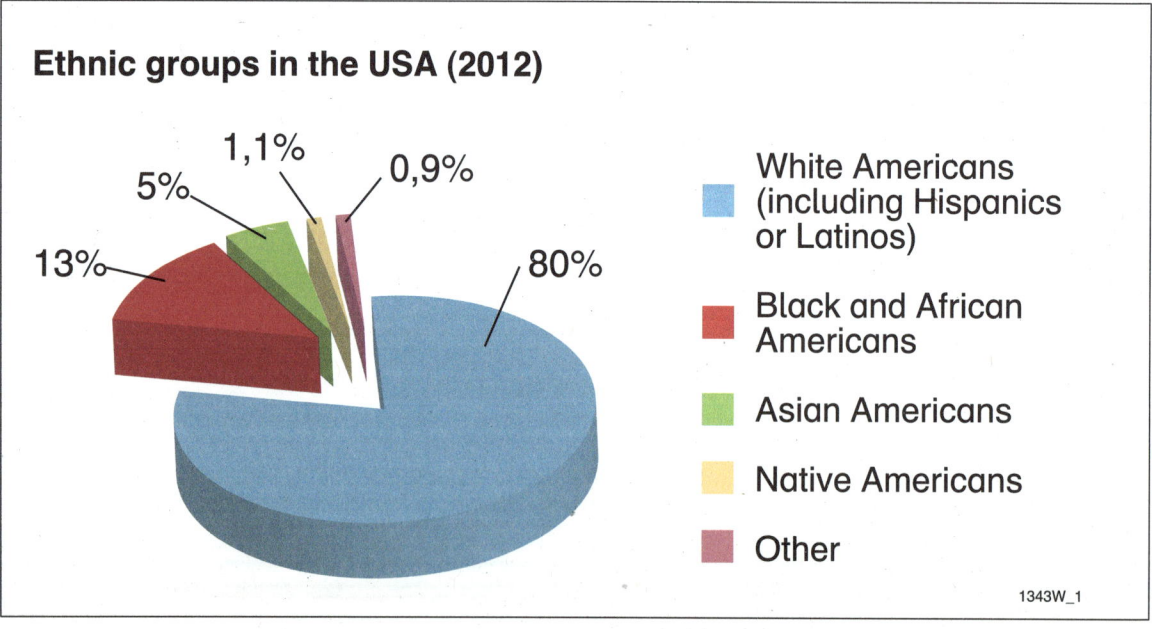

Ethnic groups in the USA (2012)

1,1%
5%
0,9%
13%
80%

White Americans (including Hispanics or Latinos)

Black and African Americans

Asian Americans

Native Americans

Other

1343W_1

Welche Bevölkerungsgruppen leben in den USA?

Wie hoch ist der Anteil der amerikanischen Ureinwohner (*Native Americans*)?

Welche Gruppe bildet die Mehrheit?

7 | A new home

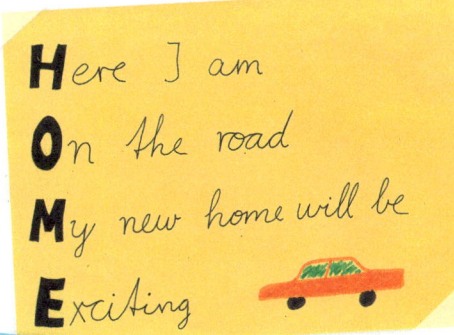

Here I am
On the road
My new home will be
Exciting

a) **Write a poem about a new home.**

6
p. 84
10
p. 85

Dein Gedicht muss sich
nicht reimen. Die Beispiel-
gedichte geben dir Ideen.
Ihr könnt das Gedicht auch
in Partnerarbeit schreiben.

My
new home.
People say "Hello.
Where are you from?"
"Germany."

Du kannst auch ein
Wörterbuch benutzen.

b) **Present it in class.**

 **Land und Leute**

Der Seefahrer Kolumbus nannte die ersten Bewohner Amerikas „Indianer", weil er bei seiner Ankunft in Amerika 1492 dachte, er sei in Indien. Die amerikanischen Ureinwohner (*Native Americans*) lebten in verschiedenen Stämmen mit eigenen Sprachen und Kulturen. Als sich weiße Siedler ab dem 17. Jahrhundert in Amerika niederließen, mussten die *Native Americans* gegen sie kämpfen, um ihre Länder und ihre Lebensweisen zu verteidigen. Viele von ihnen wurden gezwungen, ihr Land zu verlassen und in Reservaten zu leben. Reservate sind Gebiete, die *Native Americans* vor langer Zeit zugewiesen wurden, weil sie dort leben sollten. Nicht wenige *Native Americans* leben auch heute in Reservaten. Sie pflegen ihre Traditionen und versuchen, sie für ihre Nachfahren zu erhalten.

In welchem Zusammenhang hast du schon von Indianern gehört?

8 Native Americans

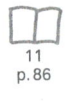
11
p. 86

Talk to your partner in German. Think about Native Americans. What do you know about them?

Die Fotos geben dir Ideen.
Denke auch an Indianergeschichten.

9 Then and now

12
p. 86/87

2
6

a) Listen and read along.

1 Native Americans lived in tribes. The young and the old lived together.

2 Some tribes lived in tepees, some lived in stone houses.

3 Some Native Americans hunted buffalos. Some went fishing. Some were farmers.

4 Some tribes had totem poles that showed pictures and told stories.

5 Pow-wows are modern events where some Native Americans dance, some sing and they all meet friends.

b) Match the pictures and the texts.

c) Write down the English words.

Die Wörter findest du in den Texten bei a).

Büffel: _____

Tipis: _____

d) Circle more words in the texts that are similar to German words.

10 A Native American

a) **Listen.**
   What did you understand?

p. 88/89

2
7

Tawny is sixteen years old. She's ...

b) **Listen again and tick.**

Drei Bilder bleiben übrig.

c) **Check with your partner.**

11 Navajo news

15/16
p.89

a) **Read the article about Tawny.**

Navajo News

This is Tawny Hale.
Her family is from the Navajo tribe.
Tawny is 16 years old and goes to
Salazar High School.
Tawny wants to be a spokesperson
for the Navajo tribe. She wants to help the
Navajo people who live on reservations.
Many can't find jobs and don't have money.
Some are very ill.
So Tawny wants to make life better.

b) **Read the questions.**
Then underline the answers in the article.

1. Which tribe is Tawny from? un

2. What does Tawny want to be? un

3. Where do some of the Navajo people live? un

4. What problems do some members
   of the Navajo tribe have? un

c) **Check with your partner.**

Um einen Text besser zu verstehen, hilft es,
bestimmte Informationen zu unterstreichen.
Verschiedene Farben für einzelne Inhalte sind
da besonders gut.
So kannst du auf einen Blick sehen,
worum es im Text geht.

Complete the wordbank.

Wörter, die du mit amerikanischen Ureinwohnern
verbindest: (→ Seite 59)

– tribe _____   _____

_____   _____

_____   _____

Gründe, um auszuwandern: (→ Seite 52−55)

– not enough food _____

_____

_____

_____

_____

Englische Wörter, die im Deutschen ähnlich sind: (→ Seite 59)

– buffalo _____

_____

_____

_____

Dieses Wort fandest du am schwierigsten:

_____

Theme 5

What's up?

In diesem *Theme* ...

- erfährst du, was amerikanische Jugendliche in ihrer Freizeit machen.
- beschäftigst du dich mit amerikanischen Einkaufszentren.
- erstellst du ein Einkaufsgespräch.
- lernst du Wissenswertes über amerikanische Sportarten.
- sprichst du über deine Lieblingssportart.

1 When school's out

Play the game with your classmates.

1
p. 100

Die Spielkarten findest du bei Aufgabe IV im Anhang.

1. Form a group of three.
   Cut out the cards.

2. One of you chooses
   a card and mimes the activity.

3. The other two have to guess
   the activity.

4. The one who says the
   correct activity first wins.

2 A typical day

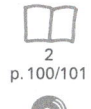
2
p. 100/101

a) Listen to Tom and
number his activities (1–4).   Zwei Bilder bleiben übrig.

 b) Circle Tom's activities.   Drei Aktivitäten bleiben übrig.

go to school by bus   go to school by car

play computer games with friends   watch TV

surf the Internet with a friend   do homework   listen to music

 c) Listen again.
Then complete Tom's sentences.

1. "On a typical day I _____."

2. "After school I _____."

3. "I often _____."

4. "In the evening I _____."

3 **Your typical day**

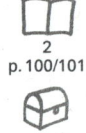
2
p. 100/101

a) **Take notes. What do you do on a typical day?**

Every morning I ...	
After school I ...	
In the evening I ...	

 b) **Write about your activities.**

Every morning I ...

_____

_____

_____

_____

_____

c) **Read out your text in class.**

So sagst du, **wie lange** du etwas tust.

    I listen to music **for 20 minutes**.

So **fragst** du, **wie lange** jemand etwas tut:

    How long do you watch TV **for**?

4 Let's go shopping

4–6
p. 102

a) Listen and tick.
Where could Cheryl and Ben go?

Zwei Antworten
sind richtig.

b) Read the plan of Wonderworld.

Places in Wonderworld Shopping Mall

1 Barney's Snack Bar   5 Books & Newspapers

2 Sam's Café   6 Fairtrade Shop

3 Sweet Corner   7 The Big Sports Shop

4 Media World

Ein Geschäft bleibt übrig.

c) Match the words and the shops.

sweets   hot chocolate   newspapers

burgers   footballs   computer games

5 A mall

a) **Design a shop. Work in groups of three.**

4
p. 102

> Du findest die Materialien bei Aufgabe V im Anhang.

1. Choose your shop, snack bar or café. Find a name for it.

2. Colour your shop, draw things or add photos.

3. Label your shop. You can look up words in a dictionary.

4. Draw people in the shop. You can also cut them out of magazines and glue them in.

5. Glue all the shops onto a poster.

> This is the Flower Shop. There are many flowers and trees. ...

b) **Present your shop in class.**

6 A picture story

7
p. 103

a) Look at the pictures. What can you see?

I'd like to buy a new T-shirt.

What about this one?

Yes, I'll try it on.

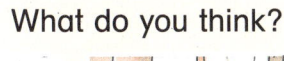

What do you think?

It's $ 30.

Yes, but I'll take it.

**b) Read the sentences.
Match the pictures and the sentences.**

1 You look great in it.

2 OK. Let's go!

3 That's expensive!

4 No, that's ugly.
Do you like this T-shirt?

5 How much is it?

2
10

c) Listen and check.

d) Make your own dialogue. Read it out in class.

Ihr könnt euren Dialog auch auf Karteikarten schreiben.

cheap • blue • nice • small •
cute • big • expensive • great • ugly • ...

7 Free time statistics

a) Read the statistics.

10
p.104

> Die englischen Zahlen findest du auf S. 124.

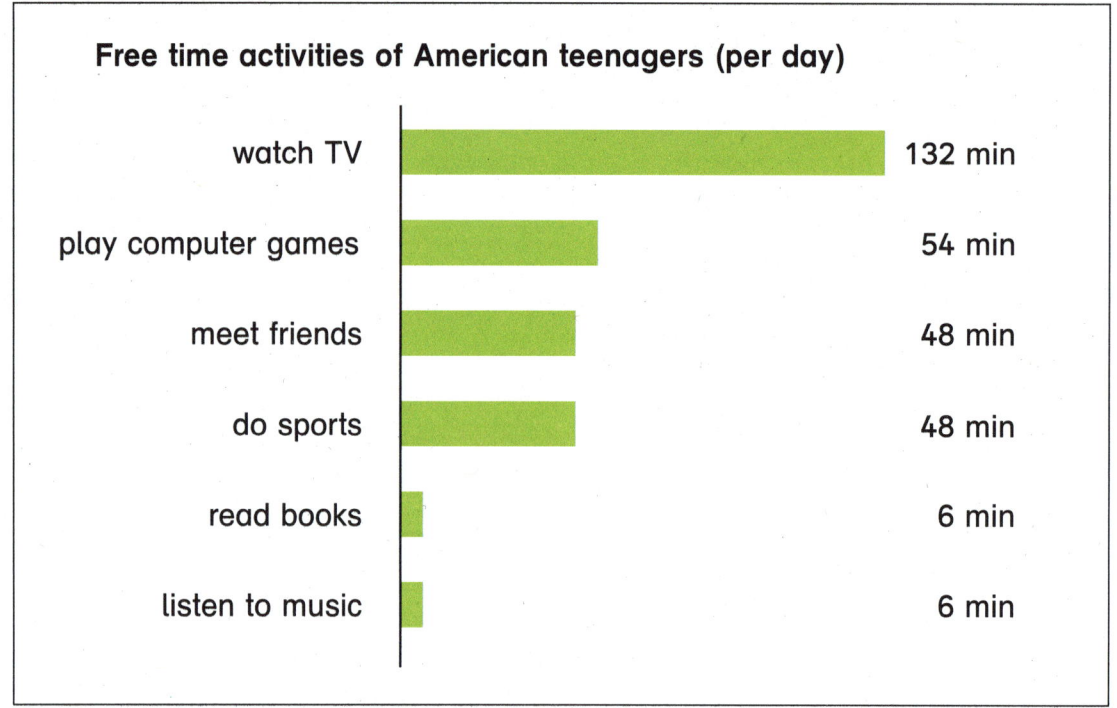

Free time activities of American teenagers (per day)

watch TV	132 min
play computer games	54 min
meet friends	48 min
do sports	48 min
read books	6 min
listen to music	6 min

b) Look at a) again. Then complete the sentences.

American teenagers _watch TV_____ for 132 minutes.

They do sports for _____ minutes.

They read books for _____ minutes.

They _____

for 54 minutes.

c) Talk to your classmates.

> What do American teenagers do in their free time?

> They meet friends.

> How long do they meet friends for?

> For 48 minutes.

8 American sports

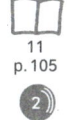

11
p. 105

2
11

a) Listen and number.

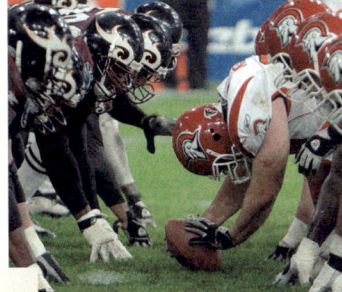

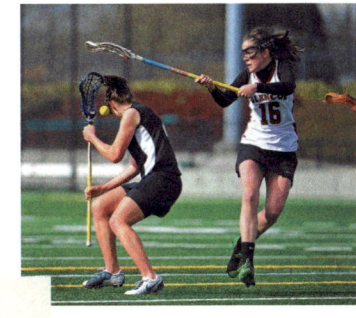

2
12

b) Listen and check.

c) Look at a) again. Write down the activities.

> do cheerleading • play baseball • play basketball •
> play ice hockey • play American football • play lacrosse

1 _____   2 _____

3 _____   4 _____

5 _____   6 _____

 d) Talk to your partner.

Have you ever tried to play lacrosse?   No, I haven't.

Have you ever watched basketball on TV?   Yes, I have.

9 **Come and join us!**

a) **Listen and read along.**

12/13
p. 106

2
13

The Lake Park News

"The Pirates" need you!

Hi, my name is Ashley Miller. I am a member of Lake Park's cheerleading group, "The Pirates." We go to all school sports events and cheer our teams on. Cheerleading is a team sport just like soccer or basketball. You have to be fit and good at sports.

We cheerleaders sing and dance. We have a lot of fun. My favorite stunt is the pyramid. I love to stand on the top.

We practice two or three times a week.

Are you interested? Come and be a cheerleader!

b) **Read the article again. Take notes.**

Name of the sport: _____

Name of the team: _____

What they do: _____

_____

Ashley's favourite stunt: _____

_____

c) **Talk to your classmates.**

What do you think about cheerleading?

It's a cool sport.

It's boring.

10 Sports, sports, sports

17
p. 109

a) Write down the words for the pictures.

b) Write down the new word.

↓ _____

Land und Leute

Sport spielt in den USA eine sehr wichtige Rolle. Manche Sportevents sind sogar nationale Ereignisse, z. B. der *Super Bowl (American Football)*. Manche Feiertage sind besonders berühmt für ihre sportlichen Höhepunkte. An Neujahr und *Thanksgiving* finden z. B. die *American Football*-Spiele der Colleges statt. Jede Mannschaft hat ihre eigenen *Cheerleaders*, die mit Schlachtrufen, Tanzen, Springen und Händeklatschen die Zuschauer zum Anfeuern animieren.
Für viele amerikanische Schüler ist es genauso wichtig, im Sport erfolgreich zu sein wie in Mathe oder Englisch.

Welche Sportarten und Sportler sind in Deutschland am beliebtesten?

11 All about American football

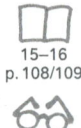

15–16
p. 108/109

a) Read the article.

"Let's talk about … American football!"

It is the most important time of the year for fans
of American football! The final game of the season
will be in February. It is a cool sport. But it is not easy!
What do you know about this famous sport?
Here are some facts:

There are two teams with eleven players.
All players wear helmets.

The teams play on a field with two
goal lines and two goals.
Each team has one goal line and a goal.

When the game starts, one team tries
to get the ball to the other goal line.
Then they get six points.

A player can also kick the ball through a goal.
Then the team gets three points.
The team with the most points wins the game.

Many Americans are crazy about football:
about 100 million people watch the final
game – the Super Bowl – on TV every year.

b) Underline the sport words in the article. un

12 Your favourite sport

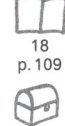
18
p. 109

a) Circle words for a presentation about your favourite sport.

Du kannst auch ein
Wörterbuch benutzen.

skates • bike • ball • puck • racket •
basketball basket • goal • helmet

dribble • kick • catch • play •
swim • throw • hit

sports field • gym • sports centre • pool

 b) Make a poster about your favourite sport.

Name of the sport: _____

What I need for my sport: _____

_____

_____

What I do: _____

_____

_____

Where: _____

_____

When: _____

_____

c) Present your poster in class.

My favourite sport is cycling.
For this sport I need a bike and ...

Complete the wordbank.

Freizeitaktivitäten: (→ Seite 64–66, 70)

– *go swimming*

_____   _____

_____   _____

Sätze, die du beim Einkaufen sagen kannst: (→ Seite 69)

_____

_____

Amerikanische Sportarten: (→ Seite 71)

– *baseball*

_____

_____

_____

_____

Wörter, die du mit Sport verbindest: (→ Seite 75)

– *kick*

_____

_____

_____

Theme 6

California

In diesem *Theme* …

- lernst du Kalifornien kennen.
- sprichst du über außergewöhnliche Berufe.
- denkst du über deinen Traumberuf nach.
- erfährst du etwas über Nationalparks in Kalifornien.
- beschäftigst du dich mit Hollywood.

1 Sounds of California

a) Listen and number.

1
p. 120

2
14

> Hinten im Buch findest du eine große USA-Karte. Wo genau liegt Kalifornien?

USA

CA

0   1000 km

b) Label the photos.

> beach • waterfall • forest fire •
> earthquake • sea lions • photographers

c) Listen and check.

2
15

d) Talk to your partner. Which photo describes California best?

> When I think of California, I think of earthquakes. What about you?

> I think of …

2 Lots to see and do in California

a) Read the information and underline:

places   activities   people   problems

Every year millions of people visit Disneyland.
You can meet Mickey Mouse and his friends there.

Park rangers help tourists in California's national parks. They look after the wild animals and nature.

There are big forest fires in California because it is often hot and windy.

Sometimes there are dangerous earthquakes in California. Then many people can lose their homes.

The Golden Gate Bridge in San Francisco is a famous sight.

People go cycling or inline skating at the beach in Santa Monica.

b) **Look at a) again.**
   Make a word web about California.

Im Internet findest du mehr Informationen.

people you can meet:

_____

_____

_____

places you can see:

_____

_____

_____

California

activities you can do:

_____

_____

_____

_____

problems:

_____

_____

_____

_____

c) **Talk to your classmates about California.**

What do you know about California?

There's … / There are …

Would you like to go to California?

Yes, I'd like to see …

No, it's too hot / expensive / dangerous / …

3 Jobs in California

3
p. 121
5
p. 123

a) **Read the page from a high school magazine.**

My dream job: stunt performer

Stunt performers often do dangerous stunts for Hollywood stars. This is why I would like to be a stunt performer. They do cool things and they often work outdoors. I am very fit and I know everything about stunts. I like that they do different stunts every day – that is great!
Roberto

My dream job: park ranger

Hi, I am Stephanie. I live in a town near Yosemite National Park. My mom works there as a park ranger. I often go to work with her at the weekends. It is a cool job! I love to work outdoors. Park rangers have to work with animals. I like that. And park rangers often help tourists. After high school I would love to be a park ranger.
Stephanie

b) **Read again. Then underline the information.
Find out about:**

1. where they work

2. what they do

3. what Roberto and Stephanie like about the jobs

Work and play

4 **A job for you?**

6
p. 123

a) **Think about <u>your</u> dream job. Take notes.**
Look at number 3 for help.

Du kannst auch ein
Wörterbuch benutzen.

indoors • outdoors • day • night • alone •
in a team • with people • with animals • with computers • …

– *where:*

– *when:*

– *with:*

b) **Write down four sentences about your dream job.**

I'd like to be …

5 **California's national parks**

7
p. 124/125

a) Read the tour flyers.

1

Come and visit California's famous
Yosemite National Park!
See beautiful plants and trees.
Visit the waterfalls and enjoy the view
from the mountains.

One-day guided tour with a park ranger
adults: $60   children (age 4–16): $45

Special offer in May: snacks for free!
Watch out! There are bears – they are very dangerous!

Tour 1

2

Feel the hot California sun in the
Death Valley National Park.
Find out about the desert and
learn its secrets.

One-day guided tour
adults: $40   children (age 6–14): $27

Visitors must bring their own drinks!
Please remember to wear caps or hats!
Watch out! There are snakes!

Tour 2

b) Match the words and the tour flyers.

mountains   bears   desert

snakes   waterfalls   California sun

c) Talk to your partner.
Which tour would <u>you</u> choose?

amazing • dangerous •
interesting • hot • cute •
big • exciting • nice •
great • …

I'd choose tour one because
I'd like to see waterfalls.
I think they are amazing.

I'd choose tour two because
I'd like to see the desert. I think it's …

6 About California

Find the words.

8
p. 125

Hollywood • Disneyland •
forest fire • earthquake •
national park • beach • waterfall

Du findest die Wörter senkrecht
und waagerecht versteckt.

D	I	S	N	E	Y	L	A	N	D	X	O	P	M	L	K
A	J	K	E	U	B	M	P	O	R	E	F	I	H	D	G
C	S	H	K	M	N	V	K	S	U	T	O	Q	A	Y	X
Q	X	R	T	K	N	G	W	A	T	E	R	F	A	L	L
N	B	P	L	R	U	C	B	J	V	N	E	P	W	H	I
G	H	G	P	B	S	R	T	Z	U	T	S	H	Z	T	R
N	Y	B	V	E	F	J	K	P	S	R	T	J	N	K	X
P	L	W	N	A	T	I	O	N	A	L	*	P	A	R	K
Q	B	V	A	C	R	S	T	Q	G	Z	F	U	J	I	X
E	A	R	T	H	Q	U	A	K	E	B	I	Z	U	I	K
X	Q	U	R	Z	T	V	I	H	A	F	R	E	T	U	S
H	O	L	L	Y	W	O	O	D	J	B	E	S	X	Y	R

7 A national park sudoku

Complete the sudoku.

7
p. 124/125

Denk dran! Alle vier Wörter müssen
– in jedem Farbfeld,
– in jeder Reihe
– und in jeder Spalte vorkommen.

bear	mountain	snake	
	waterfall		bear
mountain			snake
	snake	bear	

8 ## Visit Hollywood Film Studios!

9
p. 126
10
p. 127

a) **Read the website.**

www.museumofinventions.co.uk

Visit Hollywood Film Studios!

Tour 1: **Be ready!**

Get ready for the shock of your life:
Feel the earthquake!

Tour 2: **Be scared!**

Watch out:
on this tour you meet scary dinosaurs!

Tour 3: **Watch out!**

Meet the gorilla King Kong!
Feel your heart beat!

Extra Spanish and Chinese tours every day!

Open daily except on Thanksgiving and Christmas.
March – September: 8 am – 10 pm
October – February: 10 am – 7 pm

Prices:
1-day ticket (ages 3+): $95   2-day ticket: $119
group tickets: 10 adults $800

b) **Answer the questions in German.**

Welche Führungen
werden angeboten?

Was kostet eine Tageskarte für <u>dich</u>?

Gibt es auch eine Führung auf Deutsch?

Was hast du noch
verstanden?

9 Take a tour!

Cheryl and her family visited the Hollywood studios.

a) **Listen. Tick the correct words.**

1. They chose	Tour 1		Tour 3.
2. They went by	car		boat.
3. Cheryl saw the big	gorilla		shark.
4. She got so scared that she	screamed		laughed.
5. She bought two	CDs		DVDs.

b) **Look at number 8 again. Then talk to your partner.**

Which tour would you choose?

I'd choose tour …

Why?

It looks amazing / funny / scary / exciting / …

 **Land und Leute**

Hollywood ist als Zentrum der amerikanischen Filmproduktionen weltbekannt. Es ist ein Stadtteil von Los Angeles (Kalifornien) an der Westküste der USA. Dort befinden sich viele Fernseh- und Filmstudios, z. B. die *Universal Studios* oder *Warner Brothers*. Vielleicht hast du auch schon einmal vom *Walk of Fame* gehört. Das ist ein Gehweg in Hollywood, auf dem berühmte Künstler mit einem Stern geehrt werden. Mittlerweile sind es schon über 2500 Sterne. Auch Trickfiguren wie Donald Duck, Mickey Mouse oder die Simpsons sind hier verewigt.

Welche Hollywoodstars magst du?

10 Enjoy a movie

11
p. 127

Choose <u>one</u> cartoon. Explain it in German.

1

Hollywood - the early years.

2

11 On TV

12
p. 128

Talk to your classmates.

films • the news • talent shows • cartoons •
quiz shows • music shows • sports programmes

What do you watch on TV?

I always / often / sometimes
watch cartoons.

Do you know
a talent show on TV?

Yes, I do. I like … / No, I don't.

Would you like to be
on a talent show?

Yes! I'd like to sing / dance / …

No! I think it's crazy /
boring / too exciting / …

12 A movie poster

13
p. 128/129

Look at the poster. Answer the questions in German.

Wie heißt der Film?

Wer hat den Film produziert?

Ab wann läuft der Film?

Was hast du noch verstanden?

Ist es dir schon aufgefallen? Im **amerikanischen Englisch (AE)** werden Wörter manchmal **anders geschrieben** als im **britischen Englisch (BE)**,

z. B.: fav**o**rite (AE) — fav**ou**rite (BE)

col**o**r (AE) — col**our** (BE)

Manchmal gibt es sogar **ganz andere Wörter**:

movie (AE) — **film** (BE)

class schedule (AE) — **timetable** (BE)

Im Internet kann man leicht den Überblick verlieren.
Zum Glück gibt es Suchmaschinen. Wenn du Informationen zu einem bestimmten Thema suchst, helfen sie dir. Wichtig ist dabei Folgendes:

- Achte auf die richtige Schreibweise deiner Suchbegriffe.
- Überlege dir Schlüsselwörter, die du als Suchbegriffe nehmen kannst.
- Überprüfe immer die Informationen, die du gefunden hast.

Nicht immer ist das, was im Internet steht, richtig. Sei immer skeptisch!

13 **Your "Walk of Fame"**   Den Stern findest du auf Seite 90.

14
p. 129

a) **Make a star for <u>your</u> favourite actor, actress, singer or band.**
Start with a word web. Collect facts from the Internet.

Date of birth:

_____

Works as:

_____

_____

Lives in:

_____

_____

_____

I like him / her / them because ...

_____

_____

_____

_____

b) **Design the star.**

Jennifer Lawrence (actress)

Date of birth: 15 August 1990

Lives in Las Vegas

Greatest success: The Hunger Games

I like her because she is nice and beautiful

MY FAVOURITE BAND!

NIALL HORAN LIAM PAYNE

HARRY STYLES LOUIS TOMLINSON

COOL YOUNG

ONE DIRECTION

ALBUMS: 'TAKE ME HOME' UP ALL NIGHT', 'MIDNIGHT MEMORIES'

c) **Present your star in class.**

Complete the wordbank.

Berufe: (→ Seite 81, 82)

– park ranger

Wörter, die du mit Kalifornien verbindest: (→ Seite 78–80)

– earthquake

Fernsehsendungen: (→ Seite 87)

– sports programme

Fragen, um jemanden nach seinem Fernsehverhalten zu befragen: (→ Seite 87)

Dieses Wort fandest du am interessantesten:

A The story of the first Thanksgiving

B
p. 146/147

17

In 1620 the first English settlers, the Pilgrims[1],
came to the USA. They came by ship.
The Pilgrims wanted to find a new home in the USA.
They arrived in winter. Many of them became ill.
Some of them even died.

But then, in March, some Native Americans came to help them.
They all had food and talked a lot.
One Native American was called Squanto.
He stayed[2] with the Pilgrims. Squanto showed the Pilgrims
good places to hunt and fish.

One day the Pilgrim boy John went into the forest[3].
He got lost[4]. But some Native Americans found[5] him.
They brought John back home. The Pilgrims were very happy[6].

In 1621 the Pilgrims took the food from the fields.
They wanted to thank God and the Native Americans.
The women and children made a delicious meal with
turkey, bread, and lots of other food.
Some Native Americans came with presents.
They sang and played games for three days.

Erzähle die Geschichte
auf Deutsch nach.

---

[1] Pilgrims – Pilger
[2] stayed – blieb
[3] forest – Wald

[4] got lost – *hier:* hat sich verlaufen
[5] found – fanden
[6] were very happy – waren sehr froh

B How the raven[1] got its black feathers[2]

D
p. 151

2

18

Many, many years ago, all birds looked the same.
The raven thought that was boring.
He wanted to paint them.
So he went to the four Great Spirits[3].
He said, "I want to paint[4] all the birds.
Can you give me the paints[5]?"

The Spirits said yes. The raven said:
"But that's a lot of work. After that, paint me.
I want to be the most beautiful[6] bird." The Spirits said yes again.
Then the raven painted[7] the birds. Now they all looked different.
They were red, orange, yellow, green, and blue.

Then the raven went to the four Great Spirits and said:
"I have painted all the birds. Now you must paint me."
So the first Spirit painted the raven with great colours.
But the raven said: "That doesn't look nice."
The raven wanted to be the most beautiful bird.
So the other Spirits painted him, too.

But the raven said again: "That's not beautiful enough.
I'm not the most beautiful bird."
The Great Spirits were very angry[8] then.
They painted the raven black and
sent him back home.

This is how the raven got its black feathers.

Lies die Geschichte wie ein
Geschichtenerzähler vor.

---

[1] raven – Rabe
[2] feathers – Federn
[3] spirit – Geist
[4] paint – anmalen
[5] paints – Farben
[6] most beautiful – schönste
[7] painted – gemalt
[8] angry – wütend

Portfolio

● Das muss ich noch üben.
● Ich mache noch Fehler.
● Kein Problem!

Liebe Schülerin, lieber Schüler,

auf den folgenden Seiten findest du sechs Portfolio-Fragebögen, zu jedem *Theme* einen. Jedes Mal, wenn ihr ein *Theme* fertig bearbeitet habt, füllst du einen Fragebogen aus. So kannst du feststellen, was du schon kannst.

Das geht so: Sieh dir z. B. den folgenden Satz an.
Überlege, wie gut du das kannst, was dort beschrieben ist:

○ **Ich kann ein Gespräch über Feiertage und Feste führen.**
(→ Seite 32)

Vor jedem Satz steht ein Kreis: ○
Darunter steht die Seite,
auf der es eine Aufgabe dazu gibt:
(→ Seite 32)

Wenn du meinst, dass du das Beschriebene
schon richtig gut kannst,
dann male den Kreis grün aus: ●

Du bist dir noch nicht ganz sicher?
Dann male den Kreis gelb aus: ●

Wenn du noch große Schwierigkeiten hast,
dann male den Kreis rot aus: ●

Und jetzt: Viel Spaß!

1 Hi to high school!

American school life

○ **Ich kann eine kurze Präsentation über meinen Schulalltag halten.**
(→ Seite 17)

○ **Ich kann eine englische Website lesen und verstehen.**
(→ Seite 15)

○ **Ich kann eine Wortsammlung zum Thema Schulalltag erstellen.**
(→ Seite 16)

○ **Ich kann Unterschiede zwischen britischem und amerikanischem Englisch erkennen.**
(→ Seite 13, 14)

Acting green

○ **Ich kann einfache Sätze zum Thema Umweltschutz lesen und verstehen.**
(→ Seite 18)

○ **Ich kann ein Wimmelbild in einfachen Sätzen auf Englisch beschreiben.**
(→ Seite 18)

○ **Ich kenne einige englische Vokabeln zum Thema Recycling und Umweltschutz und kann sie richtig benutzen.**
(→ Seite 20, 21)

○ **Ich kann einen englischen Flyer selbst gestalten.**
(→ Seite 19)

2 Let's grab some food

American food

○ Ich kann verstehen, wenn Menschen erzählen,
was sie gern essen.
(→ Seite 26, 27)

○ Ich kann englische Zungenbrecher nachsprechen.
(→ Seite 25)

○ Ich kann einen englischen
Feedbackbogen verstehen und ausfüllen.
(→ Seite 30, 31)

○ Ich kann Notizen während eines Interviews machen.
(→ Seite 29)

Special days, special food

○ Ich kann ein Gespräch über Feiertage und Feste führen.
(→ Seite 32)

○ Ich kann einen Blogeintrag lesen und verstehen.
(→ Seite 33)

○ Ich kenne wichtige Feiertage, die man in den USA feiert.
(→ Seite 32)

○ Ich kann einen kurzen Text über
meinen Lieblingsfeiertag schreiben.
(→ Seite 33)

3 New places, new faces

New York

○ **Ich kann eine Tour durch Manhattan planen und sie präsentieren.**
(→ Seite 40, 41)

○ **Ich kann einen englischen Reiseführer lesen und verstehen.**
(→ Seite 37)

○ **Ich kenne berühmte Sehenswürdigkeiten in New York.**
(→ Seite 37–39)

○ **Ich kann ein Quiz zum Thema New York erstellen.**
(→ Seite 44)

Other places

○ **Ich kann Ergebnisse mit einem Partner vergleichen.**
(→ Seite 47)

○ **Ich kann eine Website zum Thema *Fairtrade* lesen und verstehen.**
(→ Seite 46)

○ **Ich kenne einige Wörter zum Thema *Fairtrade* und kann diese richtig anwenden.**
(→ Seite 46, 47)

○ **Ich kann einfache englische Sätze richtig vervollständigen.**
(→ Seite 47)

4 Finding your place

Going to America

○ Ich kann verstehen, wenn Menschen
über ihre Auswanderungsgeschichte sprechen.
(→ Seite 54, 55)

○ Ich kann ein einfaches Gedicht
zum Thema Zuhause schreiben und es präsentieren.
(→ Seite 57)

○ Ich kann kurze Texte zur
amerikanischen Geschichte lesen und verstehen.
(→ Seite 51)

○ Ich kann eine Statistik lesen und
Fragen auf Deutsch dazu beantworten.
(→ Seite 56)

Native Americans

○ Ich kann verstehen,
wenn jemand von seinem Alltag erzählt.
(→ Seite 60)

○ Ich kann einen kurzen Zeitungsartikel
verstehen und Fragen dazu beantworten.
(→ Seite 61)

○ Ich kenne einige Informationen zu
amerikanischen Ureinwohnern und ihren Kulturen.
(→ Seite 58, 59)

○ Ich kann Wörter in einem englischen
Text finden, die dem Deutschen ähnlich sind.
(→ Seite 59)

5 What's up?

Free time activities

○ **Ich kann verstehen,
wenn jemand von seinem Tagesablauf berichtet.**
(→ Seite 65)

○ **Ich kann einen Dialog im Einkaufszentrum führen.**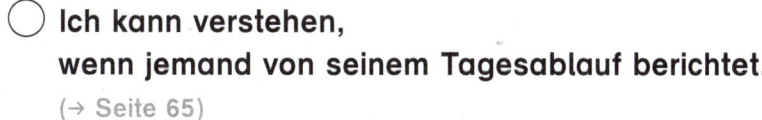
(→ Seite 69)

○ **Ich kann eine einfache Statistik
lesen und Fragen dazu beantworten.**
(→ Seite 70)

○ **Ich kann einen kurzen Text über meinen Tagesablauf schreiben.**
(→ Seite 66)

American sports

○ **Ich kann ein Gespräch über Sportarten führen.**
(→ Seite 72)

○ **Ich kann ein Poster über meine
Lieblingssportart erstellen und präsentieren.**
(→ Seite 75)

○ **Ich kann Artikel über
amerikanische Sportarten lesen und verstehen.**
(→ Seite 72, 74)

○ **Ich kenne einige amerikanische Sportarten.**
(→ Seite 71)

6 California

Work and play

○ **Ich kann ein Gespräch über Kalifornien führen.**
(→ Seite 78)

○ **Ich kann einen Tourflyer lesen und verstehen.**
(→ Seite 83)

○ **Ich kenne einige Berufe auf Englisch.**
(→ Seite 81, 82)

○ **Ich kann einen kurzen Text über meinen Traumberuf schreiben.**
(→ Seite 82)

Made in Hollywood

○ **Ich kann ein Gespräch über Fernsehgewohnheiten führen.**
(→ Seite 87)

○ **Ich kann eine englische Website
lesen und ihr Informationen entnehmen.**
(→ Seite 85)

○ **Ich kann ein englisches Filmplakat lesen und verstehen.**
(→ Seite 88)

○ **Ich kann eine Wortsammlung zu meinem Lieblingsstar erstellen.**
(→ Seite 89)

Auf den folgenden Seiten kannst du noch einmal nachschlagen, wie du etwas sagen kannst.

1

So kannst du auf Englisch **über dich selbst** Auskunft geben:

My name is Gillian.

I am fifteen years old.

I have got a cat. / **I've got** a cat.

I haven't got a dog.

2

So kannst du **über eine andere Person** Auskunft geben:

 **His** name **is** Ben.

He is from England.

He has got two sisters.

He has milk for breakfast.

 **Her** name **is** Vicky.

She is fourteen years old.

She likes hockey.

She wants to play tennis.

Weißt du noch? Bei einem **Tier** sagt man „it":

It likes milk.

3

So sagst du, ob du etwas **magst**:

😊 I **like** pizza.

☹️ I **don't like** chili con carne.

So **fragst** du, ob jemand etwas **mag**:

Do you **like** hamburgers? – Yes, I do. / No, I don't.

So **fragst** du, was jemand **besonders gerne mag**:

What is your **favourite** snack?

So **fragst** du, ob jemand schon einmal etwas **probiert** hat:

Have you ever **tried** hot dogs? – Yes, I have. / No, I haven't.

4

So kannst du ausdrücken, **wie** du etwas **findest**:

I think the food was **delicious** / **OK** / **disgusting**.

I think the music was **too slow** / **too fast**.

So kannst du sagen, was du **gerne tun würdest**:

I'd like to see the Statue of Liberty.

5

So sagst du, **wie lange** du etwas tust.

I listen to music **for 20 minutes**.

So **fragst** du, **wie lange** jemand etwas tut:

How long do you watch TV **for**?

6

So sagst du, **wie häufig** du etwas tust:

I **always** eat burgers.

I **often** eat cake.

I **sometimes** go swimming.

I **never** play baseball.

7

So sagst du, dass jemand etwas **nicht tun kann**:

I **can't** often do cheerleading.
She **can't** often do cheerleading.

So drückst du aus, dass jemand etwas **nicht hat**:

I **haven't got** a basketball.
He **hasn't got** a basketball.

So sagst du, dass jemand etwas **nicht tut** (oder z. B. **nicht mag** oder **bekommt**):

I **don't** like the poem.
She **doesn't** get a new smartphone.

8

Wenn du erzählen möchtest, **was eine andere Person über sich selbst gesagt hat**, musst du einige Wörter verändern:

I am …	–	He / She is …
My parents …	–	His / Her parents …
We lived …	–	They lived …
Our house …	–	Their house …
… for me.	–	… for him / her.

9

So kannst du ausdrücken, dass etwas **in der Zukunft passieren wird**
(z. B. morgen, nächste Woche oder nächstes Jahr):

I **will** go to Paris in June.

You **will** be fifteen next year.

So kürzt du „will" ab:

He'**ll** have a big house in ten years.

Achtung: „Will" nicht verwechseln mit dem deutschen „will" (= wollen).
Das englische „I will" heißt auf Deutsch „ich werde".

10

So kannst du erzählen, was schon **passiert ist**:

Meist hängt man an das Verb einfach ein **-ed**. Das kennst du schon!

Ben watch**ed** TV.

Das ist auch häufig bei **Fragen** so:

Have you ever play**ed** lacrosse?
Have you ever watch**ed** a basketball match on TV?

Es gibt aber auch Verben, für die du die Verbform lernen musst.

Cheryl **was** at home.	–	Cheryl **war** zu Hause.
Cheryl **got** a present.	–	Cheryl **bekam** ein Geschenk.
They **went** shopping.	–	Sie **gingen** einkaufen.

11

So sagst du, **wo genau** sich etwas befindet:

The books are **on** the table.

The caps are **in** the car.

The skateboard is **under** the table.

The poster is **near** the skateboard.

12

So kannst du beschreiben, **was es** (irgendwo) **gibt**:

There is a chair.   **There are** two chairs.

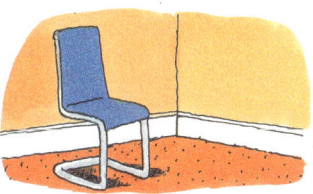   

13

So kannst du Wörter im Englischen **abkürzen**, wenn du sprichst oder z. B. eine E-Mail schreibst:

I **am** = I'**m**
I **have** got = I'**ve** got
I **will** = I'**ll**
I **would** = I'**d**

you **are** = you'**re**
they **are** = they'**re**

they **have** = they'**ve**

it **is** = it'**s**
what **is** = what'**s**
that **is** = that'**s**
there **is** = there'**s**

let **us** = let'**s**

14

So kannst du Fragen stellen:

What are your plans for the holidays?
When would you like to come?
Where do you work?
How will you get there?
How long would you like to stay?
How much do you earn?
Who is that?

15

Ist es dir schon aufgefallen? Im **amerikanischen Englisch (AE)** werden Wörter manchmal **anders geschrieben** als im **britischen Englisch (BE)**,

z. B.: fav**o**rite (AE)   –   fav**ou**rite (BE)
         col**o**r (AE)   –   col**ou**r (BE)

Manchmal gibt es sogar **ganz andere Wörter**:
     movie (AE)   –   **film** (BE)
     class schedule (AE)   –   **timetable** (BE)

A

a / an	ein(e); pro
about	über; ungefähr
across	(her)über
acting	Handeln
activity	Aktivität
action	Aktion
actor / actress	Schauspieler(in)
ad = advertisement	Anzeige, Werbung
add	zufügen
address	Adresse
adult	Erwachsene(r)
Africa	Afrika
after	nach
again	wieder, noch einmal
age	Alter
(two years) ago	vor (zwei Jahren)
all	ganz; alle(s)
alone	allein
also	auch
always	immer
am	bin
amazing	erstaunlich, toll
America	Amerika
American	amerikanisch; Amerikaner(in)
amusement park	Freizeitpark
and	und
animal	Tier
another	noch ein(e)
answer	Antwort; antworten
any	(irgend)ein
anyone	jemand
apple	Apfel
are	bist / sind / seid
arrive	ankommen
art	Kunst
article	Artikel
as	als
ask	fragen; bitten
at	in; an; um; bei
awful	furchtbar, scheußlich

B

back	zurück
bag	Tüte; Packung
banana	Banane
basket	Korb
be	sein
beach	Strand
bean	Bohne

a burger / an elective

1 activity – 2 activities

all day – den ganzen Tag

I am – ich bin
you are – du bist
he is / she is / it is –
    er ist / sie ist / es ist
we are – wir sind
you are – ihr seid
they are – sie sind

I was – ich war
you were – du warst / ihr wart

I arrived – ich kam an

bear	Bär
beat	schlagen
beautiful	schön
because	weil
become	werden
bed	Bett
before	vorher
behind	hinter, zurück
best	beste(r, s); am besten
better	besser
big	groß
bike	Fahrrad
birth	Geburt
black	schwarz
blank	leer
bling	Klunker
blue	blau
boat	Boot
book	Buch
boring	langweilig
borough	Stadtbezirk
bottle	Flasche
bought	kaufte(n)
boy	Junge
bread	Brot
breakfast	Frühstück
bridge	Brücke
bring	(mit)bringen
British	britisch
brother	Bruder
brown	braun
buffalo	Büffel
but	aber
buy	kaufen
by	mit; von

C

California	Kalifornien
call	anrufen, rufen; nennen
came	kam(en)
can / can't	können / nicht können
cap	Mütze, Kappe
car	Auto
card	Karte
catch	fangen
celebrate	feiern
central	zentral; Mittel-

because of – wegen

He is the **best** … – Er ist der beste …

leave rubbish **behind** – Müll zurücklassen

the **biggest** – der / die / das Größte

date of **birth** – Geburtsdatum

black sheep – Wort, das nicht zu den anderen passt (bei Worträtseln)

bottle bank – Altglascontainer

I **bought** – ich kaufte

a poem **by** … – ein Gedicht von …
by car – mit dem Auto

are **called** – werden genannt, heißen

Central America – Mittelamerika

change	(ver)ändern	I **changed** – ich (ver)änderte
chant	Sprechgesang	
cheap	billig, preiswert	**cheaper** – billiger
cheer on	anfeuern	
chicken	Huhn	
child	Kind	1 **child** – 2 children
Chinese	Chinesisch, chinesisch	
chips (BE) / fries (AE)	Pommes frites	
chocolate	Schokolade	hot **chocolate** – heiße Schokolade, Kakao
choose	aussuchen	
chose	suchte(n) aus	
Christmas	Weihnachten	I **chose** – ich suchte aus
cinema (BE) / the movies (AE)	Kino	
city	Stadt	
class	Klasse	in **class** – in der Klasse
classmate	Mitschüler(in), Klassenkamerad(in)	**class** schedule (AE) – Stundenplan
clean (up)	aufräumen, sauber machen	I **cleaned** – ich machte sauber
close	schließen, zumachen	
collect	sammeln	
colour	Farbe; anmalen	
come	kommen	**come** in – hereinkommen
comment	Kommentar	**Come** on! – Komm jetzt!, Mach schon!
cook	kochen	
cookie	Keks	1 **cookie** – 2 cookies
corner	Ecke	fortune **cookie** – Glückskeks
correct	richtig; korrigieren	
cost	kosten	
costume	Kostüm	
could / couldn't	konnte(n); könnte(n)/ konnte(n) nicht; könnte(n) nicht	home **country** – Heimatland
country	Land	be **crazy** about – verrückt sein nach
crazy	verrückt	
culture	Kultur	
cup	Tasse, Becher	yoghurt **cup** – Joghurtbecher
cut (out)	(aus)schneiden	
cute	süß, niedlich	
cycling	Rad fahren	

D

dad	Papa
daily	täglich
dance	tanzen
dangerous	gefährlich

date of birth	Geburtsdatum	
day	Tag	all **day** – den ganzen Tag
delicious	köstlich, lecker	
describe	beschreiben	
desert	Wüste	
design	entwerfen	
dialogue	Dialog	
dictionary	Wörterbuch	I **did** – ich tat
did / didn't	tat / tat nicht	
died	starb(en)	The dog **died**. – Der Hund starb.
different	verschieden(e)	
difficult	schwierig	
dinosaur	Dinosaurier	
disgusting	widerlich	**Don't** …! – Mache … nicht!
do / don't	tun / nicht tun	**Don't** you think …? – Denkst du nicht …?
does / doesn't	tut / tut nicht	She **doesn't** like … – Sie mag … nicht.
drama	Schauspielerei	
draw	zeichnen	
dream	Traum, Traum-	**dream** job – Traumberuf
dribble	dribbeln	
drink	Getränk; trinken	

E

each	jede(r, s)	
early	früh	
earn	verdienen	I **earned** – ich verdiente
earthquake	Erdbeben	
easy	leicht	
eat	essen	
education	Ausbildung	
Eid	Zuckerfest (muslimisches Fest am Ende der Fastenzeit)	
elective	Wahlfach	someone **else** – jemand anderes
else	sonst (noch)	
empty	leer	
energy	Energie	
English	Englisch, englisch	
enjoy	genießen	in **English** – auf Englisch
enough	genug	
entry	Eintrag	
Europe	Europa	
European	Europäer(in)	
even	sogar	
evening	Abend	in the **evening** – am Abend
ever	jemals	
every	jede(r, s)	
everybody	jede(r)	
everything	alles	

except	außer
excited	aufgeregt; begeistert
exciting	aufregend
Excuse me.	Entschuldigen Sie.
exercise book	Heft
expensive	teuer
extra	zusätzliche(r, s)

F

face	Gesicht	
fact	Tatsache	
factory	Fabrik	
false	falsch	
family	Familie	1 **family** – 2 families
famous	berühmt	
farm	Bauernhof	
farmer	Bauer / Bäuerin	
farmland	Ackerland	
fast	schnell	
father	Vater	
favorite (AE) / favourite (BE)	Lieblings-	
fed	fütterte	I **fed** – ich fütterte
feel	fühlen	
fell	fiel(en)	I **fell** in love. – Ich verliebte mich.
ferry	Fähre	
field	Feld	
fight	Kampf; kämpfen	sports **field** – Sportfeld
final	letzte(r, s)	
find (out)	(heraus)finden	**fight** for – kämpfen um
finding	Finden	
fine	in Ordnung, gut	
fire	Feuer	
first	erste(r, s); zuerst	at **first** – zuerst
fish	Fisch	the **first** … – der / die / das erste …
fishing	Angeln	
floor	Stockwerk, Etage; Fußboden	
focus	Fokus, Schwerpunkt	language in **focus** – Redemittelanhang bei *Camden Market*
folder	Schnellhefter, Mappe	
food	Essen	
football	Fußball (BE) / Football (AE)	
for	für; um; … lang	**for** you – für dich
forest	Wald	**for** help – um Hilfe
forest fire	Waldbrand	**for** three days – drei Tage lang
form	Formular; bilden	
fortune cookie	Glückskeks	
free	frei, kostenlos	

free time	Freizeit
freedom	Freiheit
fresh	frisch
fridge	Kühlschrank
friend	Freund(in)
friendly	freundlich
fries (AE) / chips (BE)	Pommes frites
from	von; aus
full	voll
fun	Spaß
funny	lustig, witzig

make **friends** – Freundschaft schließen

G

game	Spiel
garden	Garten
geography	Geografie
German	Deutsch, deutsch
get	bekommen; kommen; holen
girl	Mädchen
give	geben
glass	Glas
glue	kleben
go	gehen; fahren
goal	Tor
going	Gehen
good	gut
got	bekam(en)
grab	schnappen
great	großartig, toll
green	grün
group	Gruppe
guess	raten
guide	führen; Führer/in
gym	Turnhalle

computer **game** – Computerspiel

in **German** – auf Deutsch

I don't **get** any ... – Ich bekomme kein(e) ...
How did you **get** there? – Wie bist du dorthin gekommen?
Let's **get** some food. – Lasst uns etwas zu essen holen.

I **got** scared. – Ich bekam Angst.

greatest – größte(r, s)

guided tour – geführte Tour

H

had	hatte(n)
had to	musste(n)
half past ...	halb ... (bei Uhrzeiten)
hall	Halle
hard	schwer
has	hat; isst; trinkt
has got	hat
hat	Hut

It's **half past** four. – Es ist halb fünf.

She **hasn't (got)** ... – Sie hat kein(e, en) ...

have / haven't	haben; essen; trinken / nicht haben; nicht essen; nicht trinken	We're **having** fun! – Wir haben Spaß!
have been	bin gewesen	I **have been** swimming. – Ich bin schwimmen gewesen.
have got	haben	
have to	müssen	
he	er	**he's** come = he has come – er ist gekommen
healthy	gesund	
heart	Herz	
hello	hallo	
helmet	Helm	for **help** – um Hilfe
help	Hilfe; helfen	I **helped** – ich half
her	ihr(e); sie	
here	hier	**Here** you are! – Hier, bitte!, Bitte schön!
high	hoch	
him	ihn; ihm	
his	sein(e)	the **highest** –der / die / das Höchste
history	Geschichte	
hit	schlagen	
holiday	Urlaub, Ferien; hier: Feiertag	**home** country – Heimatland
home	Zuhause	at **home** – zu Hause
homework	Hausaufgaben	
hope	hoffen	I **hoped** – ich hoffte
hot	heiß	
house	Haus	**How** many …? – Wie viele …?
how	wie	**How** much is / are …? – Wie viel kostet / kosten …?
hungry	hungrig	
hunt	jagen	I **hunted** – ich jagte

I		
I	ich	
ice hockey	Eishockey	
idea	Idee	If I had a dog … – Wenn ich einen Hund hätte …
if	wenn	
ill	krank	
immigrant	Einwanderer / Einwanderin	
immigrate	einwandern	
important	wichtig	the most **important** – der / die / das Wichtigste
in	in, im; auf	
indoors	drinnen, im Haus	
inline skating	Inlineskaten	
be interested in	interessiert sein an	
interesting	interessant	
interview	interviewen; Vorstellungs-gespräch	I **interviewed** – ich interviewte
into	in	

Irish	irisch
is / isn't	ist / ist nicht
it	es
Italian	italienisch

It's … pounds. – Er / Sie / Es kostet … Pfund.

J

jacket	Jacke
jelly (AE) / jam (BE)	Marmelade
join	beitreten
just	genau; nur; einfach

K

keep	behalten
keyboarding	Tastschreiben am PC
kick	treten, schießen
know	kennen; wissen

L

label	beschriften
lake	See
language	Sprache
last	letzte(r, s)
later	später
laugh	lachen
learn	lernen
leave	abfahren; verlassen
left	verließ(en)
lemonade	Limonade
lesson	Stunde, Unterricht
Let's …!	Lass(t) uns …!
life	Leben
light	Licht
like	mögen; wie
line	Linie
list	Liste; auflisten
listen	(zu)hören
live	leben; wohnen
local	örtlich
locker	Schließfach
long	lang
look	(aus)sehen
lose	verlieren
a lot of, lots of	viel(e)
love	lieben, sehr gern mögen; Liebe; viele Grüße (z. B. in Briefen)
lunch	Mittagessen

at **last** – endlich

I **laughed** – ich lachte

I **learned** – ich lernte

leave behind – zurücklassen
leaving – Verlassen

I **left** – ich verließ

1 **life** – 2 lives

I **listened** – ich hörte zu

I **lived** – ich lebte

look after – sich kümmern um
look at – anschauen
look for – suchen nach
look like – aussehen wie
look up – nachschlagen
I **looked** at – ich sah … an

M

m (= metre)	Meter
made	gemacht, hergestellt
magazine	Zeitschrift
make	machen
shopping mall (AE) / shopping centre (BE)	Einkaufszentrum
man	Mann; Mensch
many	viele
map	Karte
mashed potatoes	Kartoffelbrei
math (AE) / maths (BE)	Mathe
maybe	vielleicht
me	mir; mich
meal	Mahlzeit
mean	bedeuten; meinen
meat	Fleisch
media	Medien
meet	treffen, sich treffen
member	Mitglied
memorial	Denkmal
met	traf(en)
Mexican	mexikanisch
Mexico	Mexiko
milk	Milch
mime	pantomimisch darstellen
miss	vermissen; verpassen
mistake	Fehler
mom (AE) / mum (BE)	Mama
money	Geld
month	Monat
moon	Mond
more	mehr; zusätzlich(e)
morning	Morgen
most	der / die / das meiste; am meisten
mother	Mutter
mountain	Berg
the movies (AE) / cinema (BE)	Kino
move	umziehen; bewegen
Mr (= Mister)	Herr
much	viel
mum (BE) / mom (AE)	Mama

make friends – Freundschaft schließen

1 **man** – 2 men

tribal **member** – Stammesangehörige(r)

I **met** – ich traf

I **missed** – ich vermisste, verpasste

more than – mehr als

in the **morning** – am Morgen

I **moved** – ich zog um

music	Musik
Muslim	Moslem(in); muslimisch
must	müssen
my	mein(e)

N

Native American	amerikanische(r) Ureinwohner(in)	
nature	Natur	
near	in der Nähe (von)	
need	brauchen	
never	nie	
new	neu	
New Year	Neujahr	
news	Nachrichten	
newspaper	Zeitung	
nice	schön, nett; gut	Nice to meet you. – Schön, dich kennenzulernen.
night	Abend, Nacht	
no	nein; kein	
not	nicht	
nothing	nichts	at night – am Abend, in der Nacht, nachts
now	nun, jetzt	
number	Zahl, Nummer; nummerieren	telephone number – Telefonnummer

O

of	von	special offer – Sonderangebot
offer	anbieten; Angebot	
often	oft	
old	alt	the old – die Alten
on	auf; an; in; am	
only	nur	on Mondays – montags
onto	auf	on holiday – im Urlaub
open	offen, geöffnet; öffnen	on the Internet – im Internet
or	oder	
order	Reihenfolge; bestellen	opened – geöffnet; öffnete(n)
other	andere(r, s)	
our	unsere(r, s)	
out	aus; raus	
cut (out)	(aus)schneiden	
outdoors	im Freien, draußen	
over	über	
own	eigene(r, s)	

P

page	Seite
paper	Papier
parents	Eltern
park ranger	Parkaufseher(in)
peanut butter	Erdnussbutter
pencil	Bleistift
people	Leute, Menschen
per	pro
phone	anrufen
photo	Foto
photographer	Fotograf/in
photography	Fotografie
picture	Bild
apple pie	Apfelkuchen
pirate	Pirat(in)
place	Ort
plan	planen
plant	Pflanze; pflanzen
plastic	Plastik
play	spielen
player	Spieler(in)
please	bitte
poem	Gedicht
point	Punkt
poor	arm
posted by	gepostet von
potato	Kartoffel
pow-wow	Versammlung
practice (AE) / practise (BE)	üben
present	Geschenk; präsentieren
presentation	Präsentation
price	Preis
produce	produzieren, herstellen
programme	Programm, Sendung
pupil	Schüler(in)
put	legen; stecken; steckte(n)
pyramid	Pyramide

place of birth – Geburtsort

plastic bag – Plastiktüte

I **played** – ich spielte

I **produced** – ich produzierte, stellte her

Q

question	Frage

R

racket	Schläger
railroad	Eisenbahn
read	lesen

reading	Lesen
really	wirklich
recycle	wiederaufbereiten
red	rot
remember	sich erinnern
reservation	Reservat
restroom (AE) / toilets (BE)	Toilette
rich	reich
right	Recht; rechte(r, s); rechts
room	Zimmer
rubbish	Müll
ruler	Lineal
running	Laufen, Rennen

S

said	sagte(n)	
salad	Salat	
Saudi Arabia	Saudi-Arabien	
sausage	Würstchen	
save	retten; sparen	I **said** – ich sagte
saw	sah(en)	
say	sagen	
scared	erschrocken, verängstigt	be **scared** – Angst haben
		get **scared** – Angst bekommen
scary	Furcht erregend, unheimlich	
class schedule (AE) / timetable (BE)	Stundenplan	
school	Schule	
schoolbag	Schultasche	
science	Naturwissenschaften	
scream	schreien	I **screamed** – ich schrie
sea lion	Seelöwe	
season	Saison	
secret	Geheimnis	
security officer	Sicherheitsbeamter/-beamtin	
see	sehen	
be seen	gesehen werden	
sell	verkaufen	
sentence	Satz	
settler	Siedler(in)	
shark	Hai	
she	sie	
shelf	Regal, Regal(boden)	1 **shelf** – 2 shelves
ship	Schiff	
shock	Schock	
shoe	Schuh	**shoe** size – Schuhgröße

shop	Geschäft, Laden
shopping	Einkaufen
shopping centre (BE) / shopping mall (AE)	Einkaufszentrum
short	kurz
should	sollte(n)
show	zeigen
Siberia	Sibirien
sight	Sehenswürdigkeit
sign	Schild
similar	ähnlich
sing	singen
singer	Sänger(in)
sister	Schwester
size	Größe
skate	Schlittschuh
skateboarding	Skateboarden
skyscraper	Wolkenkratzer
slave	Sklave / Sklavin
small	klein
snack bar	Imbissstube
snake	Schlange
soccer (AE) / football (BE)	Fußball
soccer ball (AE) / football (BE)	Fußball
some	etwas; einige, ein paar
sometimes	manchmal
sort	sortieren, trennen
sound	sich anhören; Geräusch
South	Süden, Süd-
Spanish	Spanisch, spanisch
speak	sprechen, reden
special	besondere(r, s)
spend	verbringen
spokesperson	Sprecher(in)
sports	Sportarten, Sport-
stadium	Stadion
stand	stehen
star	Stern
start	anfangen; Anfang
statistics	Statistik
Statue of Liberty	Freiheitsstatue
step	Stufe
stone	Stein
stood	stand(en)
story	Geschichte

show ... around – ... herumführen
I **showed** – ich zeigte

shoe **size** – Schuhgröße

sort rubbish – Müll trennen

South America – Südamerika

special offer – Sonderangebot

sports centre – Sportcenter
sports field – Sportfeld
sports goods – Sportartikel

I **started** – ich fing an

I **stood** – ich stand

student (AE) / pupil (BE)	Schüler(in)
stunt performer	Stuntman / Stuntfrau
subject	Fach
subway (AE) / underground (BE)	U-Bahn
summer	Sommer
sun	Sonne
sunny	sonnig
surf the Internet	im Internet surfen
swap	tauschen
sweet	süß
sweets	Süßigkeiten
swim	schwimmen

swimming – Schwimmen

T

table	Tabelle
take	nehmen, mitnehmen
talk	sprechen, reden
tea	Tee
teacher	Lehrer(in)
tepee	Tipi
tell	erzählen
than	als
thanks / thank you	danke
that	dass; der, die, das
That's … (= That is …)	Das ist …
the	der, die, das
their	ihr
them	sie; ihnen
theme	Thema (bei *Camden Market*: Kapitel)
then	dann
there	dort; dorthin
there is / are …	es gibt …, da ist / sind …
these	diese
they	sie (Mehrzahl)
thing	Ding, Gegenstand
think	denken, glauben
this	diese(r, s)
through	durch
throw (away)	(weg)werfen
time	Zeit
timetable	Stundenplan
tip	Tipp
tired	müde
to	zu; für; an; nach; bis
today	heute

cheaper than – billiger als

That's … pounds. – Das kostet … Pfund.

on **time** – pünktlich
three **times** – drei Mal

together	zusammen
toilet	Toilette
told	erzählte(st,n,t)
too	zu; auch
took	brachte(n)
top	Spitze
totem pole	Totempfahl
tour	Reise, Rundfahrt, Tour
town	Stadt
tree	Baum
tribe	Stamm
tried	versuchte, probierte
true	wahr
try (on)	(an)probieren
turkey	Truthahn
turn	umdrehen
typical	typisch

I **took** out the rubbish. – Ich brachte den Müll raus.

on the **top** – oben

Have you ever **tried** …? – Hast du jemals … probiert?

I **turned** – ich drehte mich um
turn off – abschalten, ausschalten

U

ugly	hässlich
uncle	Onkel
under	unter
underground (BE) / subway (AE)	U-Bahn
understand	verstehen
unfriendly	unfreundlich
up	nach oben, hinauf
us	uns
use	benutzen

can be **used** – kann gebraucht werden

V

vacation (AE) / holiday (BE)	Urlaub, Ferien
very	sehr
view	Aussicht
visit	besuchen
visitor	Besucher(in)

I **visited** – ich besuchte

W

walk	laufen; Spaziergang; Spazierweg
want	wollen
war	Krieg
was / wasn't	war / war nicht
watch	anschauen; gucken
water	Wasser
waterfall	Wasserfall
we	wir

walk away – weggehen

I **wanted** – ich wollte

I **was** – ich war

watch / **watching** TV – fernsehen, Fernsehen
Watch out! – Pass auf!

wear	tragen
weather	Wetter
week	Woche
weekend	Wochenende
welcome	willkommen
went	ging(en); fuhr(en)
were / weren't	war(st, en, t) / war(st, en, t) nicht
what	was
What's ...? (= What is ...?)	Was ist ...?
when	als; wann; wenn
where	wo; woher; wohin
which	welche(r, s)
white	weiß
who	der, die, das; wer
why	warum
will	werden
win	gewinnen
windy	windig
with	mit
without	ohne
woman	Frau
wood working	Tischlern; Werkunterricht
word	Wort
word web	Wortnetz
wordbank	Wortfeld
work	arbeiten; Arbeit
world	Welt
would	würde(st, en, et)
Would you like ...?	Würdest du gern ...?
write	schreiben

at the **weekend** – am Wochenende

I **went** – ich ging

What's up? – Wie geht's?

1 **woman** – 2 women

Y

year	Jahr
yellow	gelb
yes	ja
yoghurt	Joghurt
you	du, dich, dir; man; ihr, euch
young	jung
your	dein(e); euer / eure
yummy	lecker

... **years** old – ... Jahre alt

the **young** – die Jungen

The days of the week

Monday

Tuesday

Wednesday

Thursday

Friday

Saturday

Sunday

The months

January

February

March

April

May

June

July

August

September

October

November

December

The seasons

spring

summer

autumn

winter

Numbers

1	one
2	two
3	three
4	four
5	five
6	six
7	seven
8	eight
9	nine

9

10	**ten**
11	eleven
12	twelve
13	thirteen
14	fourteen
15	fifteen
16	sixteen
17	seventeen
18	eighteen
19	nineteen

20	**twenty**
21	twenty-one
22	twenty-two
23	twenty-three
24	twenty-four
25	twenty-five
26	twenty-six
27	twenty-seven
28	twenty-eight
29	twenty-nine

21

30	**thirty**
31	thirty-one
…	

40	**forty**
41	forty-one
…	

50

50	**fifty**
51	fifty-one
…	

60	**sixty**
61	sixty-one
…	

70	**seventy**
71	seventy-one
…	

80	**eighty**
81	eighty-one
…	

90	**ninety**
91	ninety-one
…	

100	**one hundred**
101	one hundred and one
…	

1 Hi to high school!

American school life

1.	2	School words
2.	3a)	American school life
3.	3c)	American school life
4.	5	Gillian's first day at Lake Park High School
5.	6	British or American?
6.	7	What to do?

Acting green

| 7. | 10 | Acting green at school |
| 8. | 12 | Cleaning up |

2 Let's grab some food

American food

9.	3	Funny English (Phil)
10.	3	Funny English (Fred)
11.	4	Typical American food? (chili)
12.	4	Typical American food? (peanut butter)
13.	4	Typical American food? (burgers)
14.	4	Typical American food? (chicken)
15.	4	Typical American food? (chop suey)
16.	4	Typical American food? (fish)
17.	4	Typical American food? (steak)
18.	4	Typical American food? (pasta)
19.	5	Have you ever tried …?
20.	6	Super Burger

3 New places, new faces

New York

21.	1	New York City
22.	2	Things to see in New York
23.	7a)	Tourists in New York
24.	7d)	Tourists in New York

Other places

| 25. | 9 | Different lives |

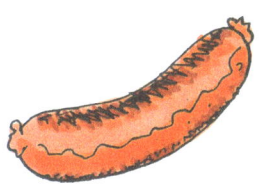

II Visit New York

III Quiz time

Zwei Karten kannst du selbst beschriften.

Which building in New York is 443 m high? (the Empire State Building)	Where is a very big zoo in New York? (in Central Park)
What is the symbol of freedom in New York? (the Statue of Liberty)	What is famous for its very big ads in New York? (Times Square)
Where are many Chinese restaurants in New York? (in Chinatown)	Where in New York was the World Trade Center? (at Ground Zero)
_____ _____ _____ _____	_____ _____ _____ _____

CAMDEN
MARKET
4

CAMDEN
MARKET
4

CAMDEN
MARKET
4

CAMDEN
MARKET
4

CAMDEN
MARKET
4

CAMDEN
MARKET
4

CAMDEN
MARKET
4

CAMDEN
MARKET
4

IV When school's out

Zwei Karten kannst du selbst beschriften.

do judo		go swimming	
go skateboarding		play basketball	
play football		go cycling	
play tennis		go running	
play hockey		listen to music	
play video games		surf the Internet	
meet friends		watch TV	
go shopping		read a book	
_____		_____	

CAMDEN MARKET 4

CAMDEN MARKET 4

CAMDEN MARKET 4

CAMDEN MARKET 4

CAMDEN MARKET 4

CAMDEN MARKET 4

CAMDEN MARKET 4

CAMDEN MARKET 4

CAMDEN MARKET 4

CAMDEN MARKET 4

CAMDEN MARKET 4

CAMDEN MARKET 4

CAMDEN MARKET 4

CAMDEN MARKET 4

CAMDEN MARKET 4

CAMDEN MARKET 4

CAMDEN MARKET 4

CAMDEN MARKET 4

Audio-CD:

westermann GRUPPE

© 2016 Bildungshaus Schulbuchverlage
Westermann Schroedel Diesterweg Schöningh Winklers GmbH
www.westermann.de

Listening texts are produced by John Green and recorded by Tim Woolf, London. Speakers: Brian Bowles, Sin Fey Chen, DeNica Fairman, James Goode, John Hasler, Helen Johns, Rebecca Lawson-Turner, Rachael Miller, Rhonda Miller, Walter Plinge, Christopher Ragland, Penny Rawlins, Martin Sherman.

Song:
CD 1: 19   Have you ever tried ...? Recorded and arranged by Tim Woolf, London. Produced by John Green.

Bildquellen:

|A1PIX - Your Photo Today, Ottobrunn: 50. |action press, Hamburg: ZUMA PRESS INC. 79. |akg-images GmbH, Berlin: Forman 58. |alamy images, Abingdon/Oxfordshire: Accent Alaska.com 27; ACE STOCK LIMITED 23, 32; Ann E Parry 36; Baker, Darren 27; BeeJay Images 36; Cheadle, Chris 93; Crabbe, Gary 77, 79; Crum, John 59; Daemmrich, Bob 10; Dagnall, Ian 58; David Cole 78; dbimages 50; Degginger, Phil 11; Design Pics 52; Grimm, Michele and Tom 85; H. Mark Weidman Photography 71; Hasenkopf, Juergen 42; Haviv, Joshua 3; Hellerstein, Steve 23; Henry Westheim Photography 27; Hoff, Dana 6; Kord, Russel 39; M Stock 72; Megapress 26; Mike Booth 77, 85; Nic Cleave Photography 37; OJO Images Ltd 27, 32; Rhodes, Ed 79; RM USA 85; Robinson, Leena 53; Skold, Fredrik 71; Stockbroker 32; Visions of America 63, 73; Wall, David 51. |Bildagentur Geduldig, Maulbronn: 49, 59. |Bildagentur Schapowalow, Hamburg: Harding, Robert 36. |bildagentur-online GmbH, Burgkunstadt: 59. |CartoonStock.com, Bath: 87. |Colourbox.com, Odense: 42; Giovanni 39. |Daugsch, Britta, Heidelberg: 10, 10, 10, 20, 58, 87. |dsphotos.de, Hamburg: Titel. |F1online digitale Bildagentur GmbH, Frankfurt/M.: RFJohner 50. |FAIRTRADE Österreich, Wien: 47. |fotolia.com, New York: Arcurs, Yuri 26; babimu 6; bradleyhebdon 54, 55; Delphimages 35; ExQuisine 20; gaelj 50; grafikplusfoto 50; Jgz 50; Kitty/ Neudert, Kati 52; mandritoiu 38; Monkey Business 10, 15; noel moore 37; rabbit75_fot 78; rdnzl 20. |Getty Images, München: Chapon, Jean Claude 46; Sugar, Jim 79; The Washington Post 11. |Glow Images GmbH c/o Regus, München: Visions of America/ Purestock 37. |Herzig, Reinhard, Wiesenburg: 59. |Imago, Berlin: McPHOTO/Baumann 50. |Interfoto, München: Science & Society/ Past Pix 59. |iStockphoto.com, Calgary: 20; Anderson, James 36; anouchka 39; Brown, Anthony 42; Brown, Matt 74; carlosalvarez 86; chris scredon 6; Churchill, Robert 12; Davel5957 77; DesignerforU 38; ferrantraite 52; JulNichols 15; Lya_Cattel 42; Michael Krinke Photography 36; Nikiforov, Michael 39; ozgurdonmaz 26; peeterv 38; Plougmann 54, 55; stellalevi 79; Wiese_Harald 79. |Kobal Collection, Berlin: AMERICAN ZOETROPE / Kobal Collection / images.de 88. |Kulling, Annika, Braunschweig: 57, 57. |laif, Köln: Piepenburg 81; Sasse 37. |Lookphotos, München: Heeb 58. |OKAPIA KG - Michael Grzimek & Co., Frankfurt/M.: J-L Klein & M-L Hubert 50. |PantherMedia GmbH (panthermedia.net), München: arina habich 32; Eder, Hans 58; Heiber, Werner 37. |Picture-Alliance GmbH, Frankfurt/M.: 8, 51; All Canada Photos/Cheadle, Chris 50; AP Images/Sammy Jo Hester 11; AP/Humphrey, Mark 74; DOUG BEGHTEL 9, 11; dpa/dpaweb/Sports&news 81; dpa/EPA/da Silva, Peter 78; dpa/Humphreys 78; dpa/Scheidemann, Achim 71; imagestate/HIP/Ann Ronan/Picture Library 49, 51; moodboard 26; newscom/Bryan Yablonsky 63, 74; Newscom/SIPA USA 37; ZB/W. Thieme 45. |REUTERS, Berlin: 32. |Schenden, Laurie, Santa Monica: 61. |Shutterstock.com, New York: 20, 20, 42, 90; ABB Photo 53; Doug, James 71; Heap, Steve 78; James A Boardman 71; Perugini, William 36; photosthatrock 71; Silver, William 83; somyot pattana 54, 55. |stock.adobe.com, Dublin: Eléonore H 50. |TransFair e.V., Köln: 46, 46; Oliver Scheel 46. |Trebels, Rüdiger, Düsseldorf: 56. |ullstein bild, Berlin: AP 78; Granger Collection 92; JOKER/Eglau, Katharina 32. |Westend 61 GmbH, München: Fotofeeling 83. |www.offthemark.com, Melrose: 87.
Einleger: |Alamy Stock Photo (RMB), Abingdon/Oxfordshire: Haviv, Joshua 3.2; Nic Cleave Photography 3.1; Pavone, Sean 3.3. |fotolia.com, New York: nikla 3.6. |Picture-Alliance GmbH, Frankfurt a.M.: Newscom/SIPA USA 3.4. |ullstein bild, Berlin: 3.5.

Welcome!

Den *Camden Market* kennst du ja schon aus dem letzten Jahr. Das ist ein Straßenmarkt in London. Nach ihm ist dieses Buch benannt.

Im *Camden Market Arbeitsheft Inklusion 2* findest du sechs *Themes* mit vielen spannenden Übungen zu Themen wie Tiere, Geburtstage, Berufe und vieles mehr.

Die Hauptpersonen heißen Gillian, Rajiv, Caroline, Charlie und Karla. Sie kommen aus Großbritannien. Du wirst viel über sie und ihr Leben in England erfahren.

Viel Spaß beim Englischlernen!

Gillian Collins
- is 12 years old
- her birthday is in April
- lives with her mum
- has got a cat
- likes football and animals

Rajiv Patel
- is 12 years old
- his birthday is in February
- his family is from India
- his parents have got a shop
- likes hockey and music

Caroline Lambraki

- is 12 years old
- her birthday is in May
- has got a brother
- has got a rabbit and a dog
- likes football and music

Charlie Batson
- is 12 years old
- his birthday is in June
- has got two sisters
- has got a goldfish
- likes football

Karla Marshall
- is 13 years old
- her birthday is in October
- has got a brother
- has got a rabbit
- likes basketball

Inhalt

Wegweiser

Symbole und Verweise

Diese Dinge übst du:

 Hören

 Sprechen

 Wortschatz

 Lesen

 Schreiben

 Hier kannst du auf Deutsch z. B. über englische Schilder sprechen.

 Diese Aufgabe ist ein bisschen schwieriger.

 Dieser Text ist auf CD.
4

Hier gibt es eine thematisch passende Aufgabe im
Camden Market Textbook.
Die obere Zahl nennt die Aufgabennummer,
die untere die Seitenzahl.
9
p. 40

Wörter in grauer Schrift kannst du in deinen eigenen Sätzen austauschen.

Diese Kästen werden dir im Buch begegnen:

 Hier erfährst du interessante Dinge über Großbritannien.

 Hier findest du wichtige Redemittel.

 Hier findest du Tipps zum Englischlernen.

 Hier bekommst du Tipps zu den Aufgaben.

Theme 1

After the holidays

In diesem *Theme* ...

- übst du, von deinen Ferien zu erzählen.
- lernst du die Landesteile Großbritanniens kennen.
- findest du Unterschiede und Gemeinsamkeiten von britischen und deutschen Schulen heraus.
- berichtest du über deine Schule.

1 Holidays

Look at the pictures. What can you do in your holidays?
Match the pictures and the sentences.

1 You can go to the beach.

2 You can go swimming.

3 You can go to a farm.

4 You can read comic books.

5 You can go to an interesting city.

2 Back home

a) Listen. Where was Charlie?

in Cornwall   in London   in Berlin

b) Listen again. Find the correct order (1–4).

Hi Charlie!

It was rainy.

Where did you go on holiday?

I had ice cream every day.

What did you do?

Hi Caroline!

What was the weather like?

I was on a campsite in Cornwall.

c) Act out the dialogue with your partner.

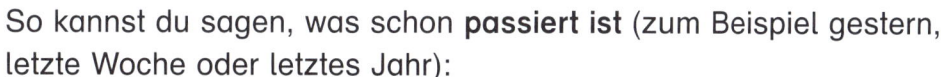

So kannst du sagen, was schon **passiert ist** (zum Beispiel gestern, letzte Woche oder letztes Jahr):

> I **had** ice cream every day.
> It **was** rainy.
> Karla **played** basketball.
> Rajiv **went** to Camden Market.

Fragen stellst du so:

> Where **was** Charlie?
> What **did** you do?

3 Holiday activities

3 p.16

2–3

a) Listen. What is it about?

Du musst nicht jedes Wort verstehen, um die Aufgabe zu lösen.

holidays

food

b) Listen again and match.

Eine Denkblase bleibt übrig.

Karla

George

1

2

3

4 I was …

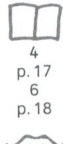
4 p.17 6 p.18

Talk to your partner. Look at number 2 for help.

Where did you go on holiday?

I was at home / went to England.

What did you do?

I played basketball.

What was the weather like?

It was sunny.

5 Rajiv

5
p.17

a) Match the words and the pictures.

1 angry   2 happy   3 sad

 b) Read and tick.

Rajiv is   angry.   happy.   sad.

Thursday, 2 August

Today was GREAT!

I like the holiday postcard from Caroline.

It's really cool.

I went to Camden Market with Charlie today.

They had cool T-shirts there.

Then we had pizza. ☺

---

 c) Read again. Is it true or false?

	true	false
1. The text is from Tuesday.		
2. Rajiv likes the holiday postcard from Caroline.		
3. Rajiv and Charlie went to Portobello Market.		
4. Then they had cake.		

 **Land und Leute**

Wusstest du, dass das Vereinigte Königreich (*United Kingdom*) aus den Landesteilen England, Schottland (*Scotland*), Wales und Nordirland (*Northern Ireland*) besteht? Alle Teile haben ihre Besonderheiten und sind stolz auf die eigenen Traditionen. Daher solltest du zum Beispiel Schotten auch nie als Engländer bezeichnen. Das passt nur für die Bewohner von England.

In Deutschland heißen die Landesteile Bundesländer. Welche kennst du?

6   A word search

7
p. 18

Find the words.

Suche nach Hobbys und Wetterwörtern.

1	B	A	S	K	E	T	B	A	L	L
2	J	R	S	N	O	W	Y	K	O	W
3	L	V	A	X	R	A	I	N	Y	M
4	S	U	N	N	Y	D	C	K	T	O
5	F	O	O	T	B	A	L	L	G	H
6	I	X	S	W	I	M	M	I	N	G
7	W	I	N	D	Y	H	L	R	N	A

Manchmal möchtest du Wörter und Ausdrücke zu einem Thema sammeln. Besonders gut geht das in einem Wortnetz. Schreibe dein Stichwort in die Mitte und ordne deine Wörter darum herum an.

7 **My holidays**

7
p. 18

a) **Look at the words and the pictures.**
Make a word web about <u>your</u> holidays.

Wähle die Wörter aus, die
zu deinen Ferien passen.

I was …

_____

_____

London

– at home   – in England
– on a farm   – in Scotland
– in the park   – in London
– at the beach   – in Mannheim
– at the zoo   – …

my holidays

The weather was …

_____

_____

I played … / had …

_____

_____

– sunny
– rainy
– …

– hockey   – ice cream
– football   – …
– with the animals

 b) **Present your holidays in class.**

I was in Portugal.

The weather was sunny.

I played volleyball every day.

8 A postcard

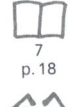

a) Read the postcard. What is it about?

holidays   birthdays   sports

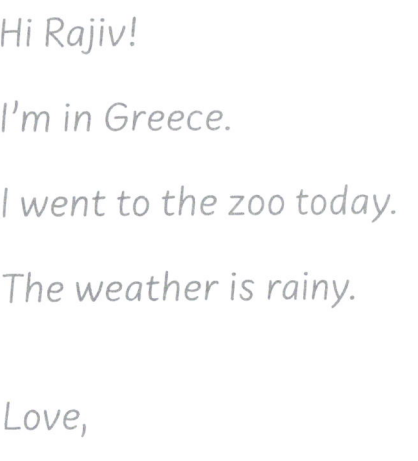

Hi Rajiv!

I'm in Greece.

I went to the zoo today.

The weather is rainy.

Love,

Caroline

Rajiv Patel

b) Write a postcard to your partner. Look at a) for help.

Hi _____!

I'm in _____.

I _____

_____.

The weather is _____.

Love,

_____

 c) Let your partner read your postcard.

9 At school

9/10
p. 19

4

a) Listen and tick.   Ein Schulfach bleibt übrig.

English   biology   geography   science

maths   PE   French   history

German   art   ICT   music

b) Listen again and look at a).
Circle Rajiv's new subjects.

c) Which subjects do <u>you</u> have?

I've got French.
I don't have ICT. …

10 Haverstock School

p. 20/21

a) Look at the website. Talk about it in German.

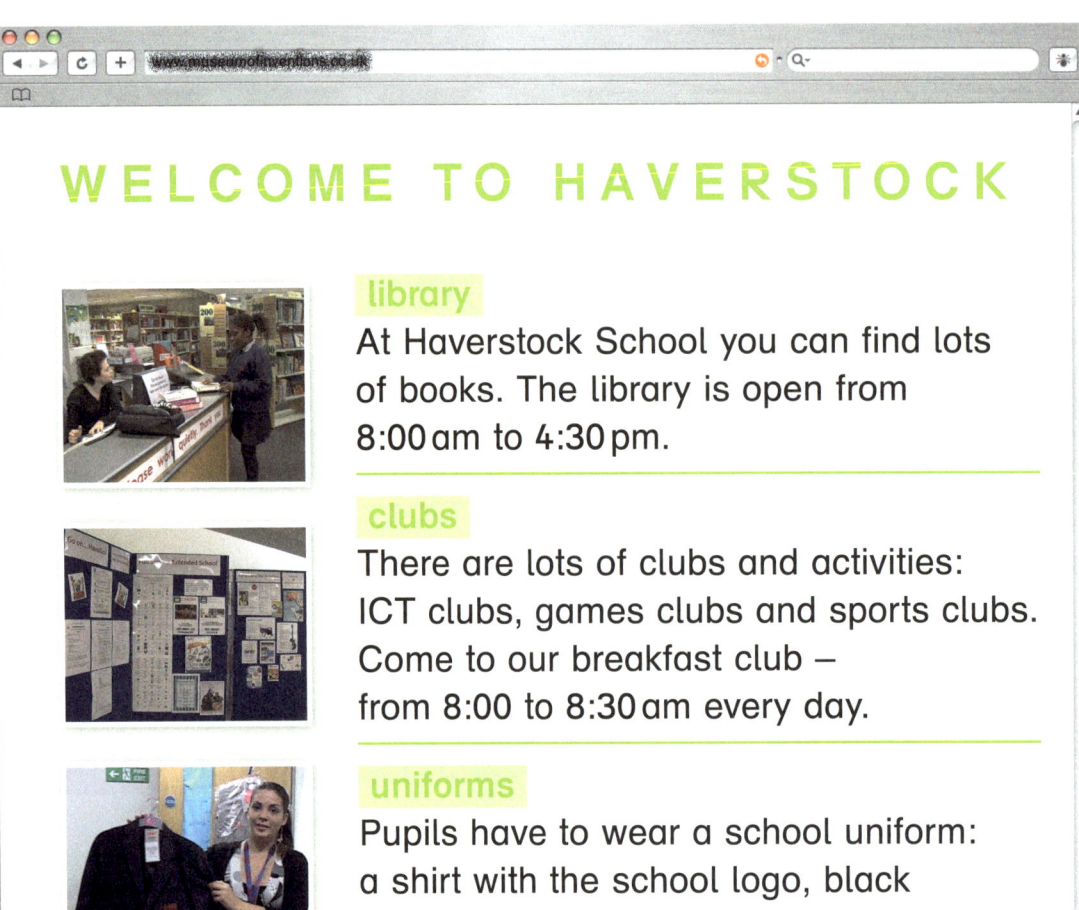

www.museumofinventions.co.uk

WELCOME TO HAVERSTOCK

library
At Haverstock School you can find lots of books. The library is open from 8:00 am to 4:30 pm.

clubs
There are lots of clubs and activities: ICT clubs, games clubs and sports clubs. Come to our breakfast club – from 8:00 to 8:30 am every day.

uniforms
Pupils have to wear a school uniform: a shirt with the school logo, black trousers or skirts and black shoes.

 b) Read the website. Is it true or false?

	true	false
1. At Haverstock school there is a library.		
2. The breakfast club is from 8:00 to 9:30 am.		
3. Pupils wear a school uniform with the school logo.		

 **c) Talk to your partner in German.**
What about your school? What is different?

11 A new classmate

 14
p. 22

 5

Listen and number (1–6).

NICK

LISA

JIM

London

Manchester

Cardiff

12 In class

14
p. 22

a) Match the questions and the answers.

What's your name?

1

Playing football.

How old are you?

2

In April.

When is your birthday?

3

Green.

Where are you from?

4

Gillian.

What's your hobby?

5

I'm twelve years old.

What's your favourite colour?

6

I'm from Camden.

b) Listen and check.

Mit dem Spiel in Aufgabe I im Anhang kannst du üben.

c) Read out the dialogue with your partner.

So kannst du **Fragen stellen**:

What's your hobby?
When is your birthday?
Where are you from?
How old are you?

13 Your dialogue

14
p. 22

Make your own dialogue. Look at number 12 for help.

 **Land und Leute**

Britische Kinder kommen in die Schule, wenn sie fünf Jahre alt sind. Die Kinder gehen sechs Jahre zur Grundschule. Danach besuchen die Schüler eine weiterführende Schule, z.B. eine Gesamtschule. Auch die *Haverstock School* ist eine Gesamtschule.

In vielen Schulen beginnt der Tag mit der *registration*. Hier wird die Anwesenheit überprüft. Einmal in der Woche gibt es eine Schulversammlung, bei der wichtige Ankündigungen gemacht werden. Hier erfahren die Schüler alles über Projektwochen, Sportveranstaltungen, Theateraufführungen und vieles mehr.

Was würdest du über Schulen in Deutschland erzählen?

So kannst du über **mehrere Personen** oder **Dinge** sprechen:

My favourite teachers **are** Mr Black and Mrs Khan.

The school rules **are** great.

14 A word web

15
p. 23

Make a word web about <u>your</u> school.

Du kannst deine Lehrkraft
nach weiteren Wörtern fragen.

– my school's name:

_____

_____

– school clubs:

_____

_____

_____

my school

– my favourite teachers:

_____

_____

– my favourite subjects:

_____

_____

_____

– other things:

_____

_____

_____

15 My school

15
p. 23

a) Make a poster about your school. Look at number 14 for help.

The name of my school is _____

_____.

The school clubs are _____

_____

_____

_____.

My favourite teachers are _____

_____.

My favourite subjects are _____

_____

_____.

Other things: *There is ...* _____

_____

_____.

 b) Present your poster in class.

Complete the wordbank.

Sätze, um jemanden nach seinen Ferien zu fragen: (→ Seite 9, 10)

– Where did you ...

_____

_____

Sätze, um über die Ferien zu berichten: (→ Seite 9, 10)

– I was ...

_____

_____

_____

Wörter, um über die Vergangenheit zu sprechen: (→ Seite 9)

– was

_____

_____

Schulfächer: (→ Seite 15)

– French _____ _____

_____ _____

_____ _____

Theme 2

Around London

In diesem *Theme* ...

- lernst du viele Londoner Sehenswürdigkeiten kennen.
- übst du, Wegbeschreibungen zu verstehen und zu geben.
- schreibst du über London und deine liebsten Sehenswürdigkeiten.
- sprichst du über Zootiere.

1 Pictures

p. 34–37

a) Look at the pictures. Where is it?

b) Listen and number (1–5).

7

2 New friends

1
p. 34/35

8

a) Listen and read along.

What would you like to see in London?

Hello Gillian! This is my friend Rob.

Hi Rob! Where are you from?

I'd like to see Tower Bridge!

OK! Let's take the bus! We can go on a tour.

I'm from Manchester.

Yes, that's great.

b) Act out the dialogue.

3 Some sights

a) **Read the information.**

1
p. 34/35

Die Informationen kannst du dir hier anhören: 9

Welcome to London!

A

Hyde Park

Visit the park and have fun! You can have a picnic and sit in the sun.

B

The Tower of London

Visit London's famous castle and see the towers.

C

Buckingham Palace

The Queen lives here when she is in London.

 b) **Match the photos and the texts.**

 c) **Check with your partner.**

4 Sightseeing in London

Auf der Karte auf Seite 131 siehst du, wo die Sehenswürdigkeiten liegen.

a) **Listen and point.**

3
p. 36/37
8
p. 40

10

b) **Listen again and number (1–7).**

the London Eye

Big Ben

Tower Bridge

The London Tour

Buckingham Palace

Hyde Park

Madame Tussauds

London Zoo

Land und Leute

London kann man sehr gut mit dem Bus erkunden. Es gibt viele Doppeldecker-busse, von denen man eine tolle Aussicht hat. Viele Touristenbusse sind oben offen.

Es gibt auch andere wichtige Verkehrsmittel in London, darunter die U-Bahn und viele Taxis. Aber Vorsicht! In Großbritannien gilt Linksverkehr. Das heißt, dass alle Autos auf der linken Straßenseite fahren müssen. Beim Überqueren der Straße muss man als Fußgänger deshalb zuerst nach rechts schauen.

Kennst du noch andere Länder, in denen Linksverkehr gilt?

5 London sights

3
p. 36/37
8
p. 40

11

a) Listen and read along.

Pass gut auf: Es sind nicht alle Sätze aus dem Hörtext abgedruckt.

They've got lots of animals.
1

Madame Tussauds

You can see lots of famous people here – but in wax.
2

the London Eye

It's a big park.
3

Buckingham Palace

The Queen lives here.
4

Hyde Park

It's a famous tower.
5

London Zoo

From the top you can see lots of famous sights.
6

Big Ben

It's a famous bridge over the Thames.
7

Tower Bridge

b) Match the sentences and the sights.

Wenn du etwas auf Englisch hörst, musst du nicht alles verstehen.
Achte auf Wörter, die du bereits kennst.
Auch die Hintergrundgeräusche können dir helfen.
Daraus kannst du oft schließen, wo sich die Sprecher befinden.
Höre dir den Text auch immer mehrmals an.
Dann kannst du ihn besser verstehen.

6 Your favourite sights

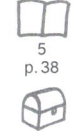
5
p. 38

a) Make a list of your
   top three London sights.

Die Aufgaben 3–5 geben dir
Ideen. Sie zeigen dir auch,
wie man die Wörter schreibt.

My top three London sights:

—

—

—

b) Read the dialogue and act it out. Then make your own dialogue.

What would you like
to see in London?

I'd like to see
Madame Tussauds.

What about
London Zoo?

Yes, that's interesting / great, too.

And what about
Hyde Park?

No, that's boring.

So kannst du sagen, was du **gerne tun würdest**:
   I'd like to see Madame Tussauds.

So kannst du ausdrücken, **wie** dir etwas **gefällt**:
   ☺ That's **great / interesting**.
   ☹ That's **boring**.

So sagst du, **in welche Richtung** jemand gehen soll:

Turn left into Park Street.

Turn right into School Road.

Go straight on.

So **fragst** du nach dem Weg:

Excuse me, please. How can I get to the supermarket?

---

7 **How can I get there?**

6
p. 39
7
p. 40

12–14

a) Listen. Find the routes on the map.

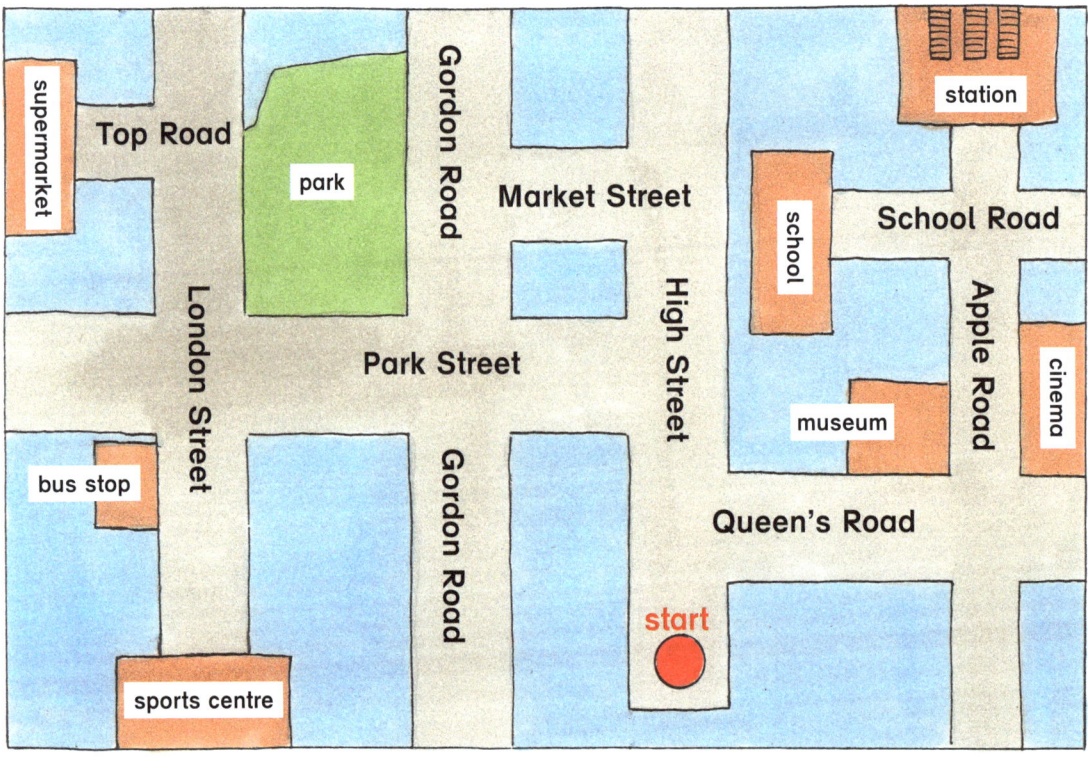

supermarket

Top Road

park

Gordon Road

Market Street

station

school

School Road

London Street

Park Street

High Street

Apple Road

cinema

museum

bus stop

Gordon Road

Queen's Road

start

sports centre

b) Listen again and look at the map. Where are the people in the end?

1. The woman is at the _____.

2. The man is at the _____.

3. The child is at the _____.

8 Where is Rob?

6
p. 39

a) **Read the dialogue.**

Caroline:	Where's Rob?
Gillian:	Oh no, we lost him! Let's phone him.
Caroline:	Good idea!
Rob:	Hello?
Caroline:	Hi, Rob! It's Caroline. Where are you?

…

15

b) **Listen and look at the map.
Where is Rob in the end?**

Rob is at …

Madame Tussauds. the Sherlock Holmes Museum.

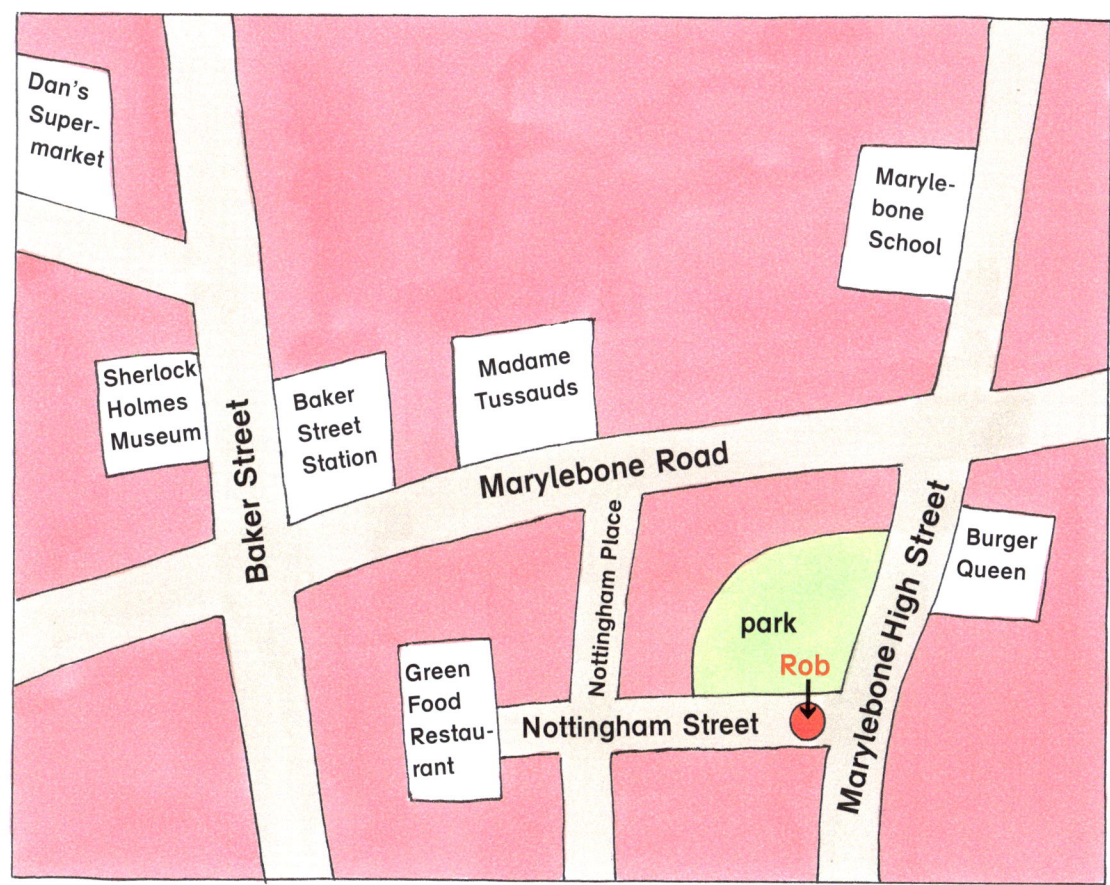

9 Excuse me, please!

7
p. 40

a) Work with your partner. Play the game in class.

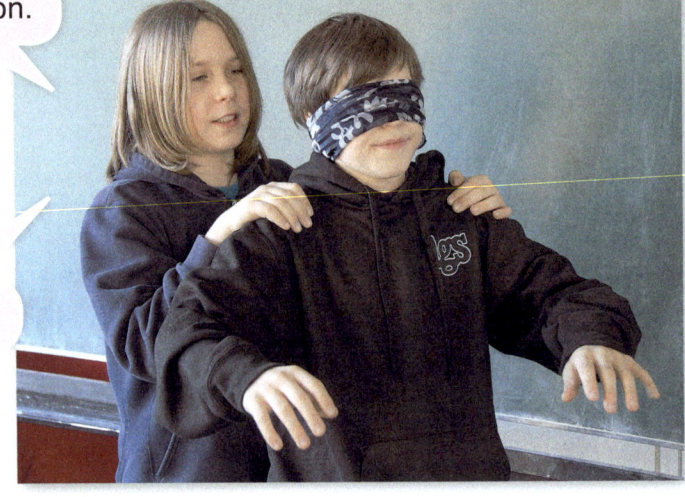

Go straight on.

Turn right.

**b) Look at the map in number 7 again.
Ask your partner.**

Zum Nachfahren der Wege könnt
ihr einen Radiergummi nehmen.
Fangt beim „Start"-Feld an.

Excuse me, please.
How can I get to the station?

Go straight on.
Turn right into ... Then ...
Then you're at the ...

10 In London

p. 38–40

**Look at the photo.
Explain it in German.**

11 A London rap

8
p. 40

16

a) Listen and read along.

A trip to London, oh that's fun!

Come on, let's go now, everyone!

I'd like to see Big Ben today.

In London, London! London, hey!

★

A trip to London, oh that's fun!

Come on, let's go now, everyone!

I'd like to see Tower Bridge today.

In London, London! London, hey!

★

A trip to London, oh that's fun!

Come on, let's go now, everyone!

I'd like to see Buckingham Palace today.

In London, London! London, hey!

b) Complete the rap. Then speak it in class.

Madame Tussauds • the London Eye • London Zoo • Hyde Park

A trip to London, oh that's fun!

Come on, let's go now, everyone!

I'd like to see _____ today.

In London, London! London, hey!

12 A London poster

Du kannst Sehenswürdigkeiten malen. Oder drucke sie aus und klebe sie auf.

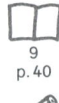

9
p. 40

a) **Make a poster about London.**
   Look at number 3−5 for help.

London

London is in _____.

My favourite sight is _____

_____.

I like _____, too.

It is _____.

_____ is boring.

I'd like to _____

_____ in London.

---

b) **Present your poster in class.**

13 Zoo animals

a) Match the photos and the words.

10
p.41

Win two tickets to London Zoo!

1

2

3

4

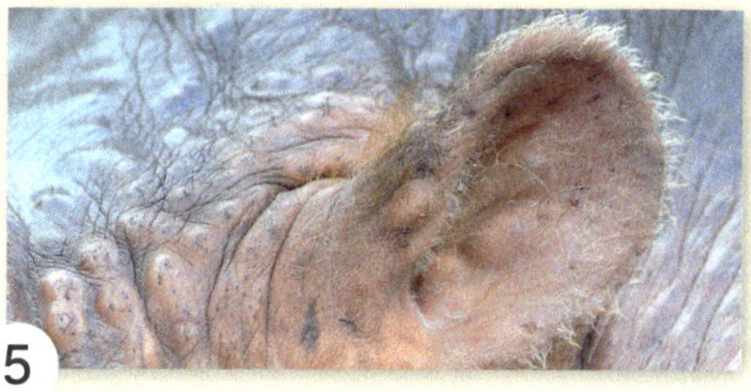

5

6

hippo

lion

penguin

tiger

gorilla

zebra

17

b) Listen and check.

14 A tiger in London

am ist eine Uhrzeit am Vormittag.
pm ist am Nachmittag oder Abend.

a) Listen and read along.

4 pm: At London Zoo

4:30 pm

5 pm: At Gillian's home

6:15 pm

b) Match the sentence parts.

Eine Uhrzeit bleibt übrig.

1. The tiger is at the park

2. The tiger is in the streets of London

3. Gillian's mother is back home

at 5 pm.

at 5 am.

at 4:30 pm.

at 6:15 pm.

15 **The tiger**

p. 42/43

The tiger likes the tour.

  Match the pictures and the sentences.

1

2

3

4

Ha, there are so many people!
I like Hyde Park.

Great! A tourist with
a big sandwich!

I love swimming! That's cool.

I'd like to see some famous people.
Let's go to Madame Tussauds.

🇬🇧 **Land und Leute**

Im Londoner Zoo gibt es über 750 verschiedene Tierarten. Wusstest du, dass es blaue Frösche gibt? Oder hast du schon einmal von Nacktmullen gehört? Seit ein paar Jahren gibt es aber keine Elefanten mehr im Londoner Zoo.

Um die Tiere hautnah kennenzulernen, kann man einen Tag lang *junior keeper for a day* sein. Dazu muss man 11–15 Jahre alt sein. Als *junior keeper* begleitest du einen erfahrenen Tierpfleger bei seiner Arbeit. So kannst du zum Beispiel Giraffen füttern oder Lama-Gehege ausmisten.

16 Cartoons

p. 42–45

a) Look at the cartoons.

Weißt du noch?
do not = don't

der erste = *the first*
der zweite = *the second*

b) Talk to your partner.

Which cartoon do you like best?

I like the first / the second cartoon best.

Why?

It's funny / great.

17 **Lunch for the animals**

14
p.44

19–21

a) **Listen and match.**

A   B

C   D

E   F

8 am

11 am

1 pm

2 pm

4 pm

8 pm

 b) **Check with your partner.**

When do they feed the penguins?

At …

Überlege doch mal,
was die Tiere oben
„bestellen" würden.

Menu for Monday
• fish
• meat
• plants

18 Animals are …

13
p.44

22

a) Listen and repeat.

1 strong   2 big   3 cute

4 dangerous   5 fast   6 funny

b) Talk to your classmates.

What are your favourite animals?   My favourite animals are lions.

Why?   They are strong / big / cute / dangerous / fast / funny.

19 Animal quiz

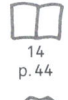
14
p.44

Read the notes.
Then play the quiz with your partner.

gorillas
– big and strong
– brown or black
– two legs
– plants

They're big and strong.   Gorillas.

They've got …   …

penguins
– small
– black and white
– two legs
– fish

tigers
– big and dangerous
– orange and black
– four legs
– meat

They eat …

…

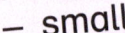

So kannst du über **mehrere Personen, Tiere** oder **Dinge** sprechen:

They eat meat.   **They have got** four legs.

20 A word search

14
p.44

a) Find the animals.

1	U	Z	E	B	R	A	B	R	I	A
2	G	X	E	P	E	N	G	U	I	N
3	O	G	O	R	I	L	L	A	V	U
4	E	O	N	T	I	G	E	R	N	K
5	M	K	A	Y	L	I	O	N	W	L
6	X	Z	L	O	Q	H	I	P	P	O

b) Write down the animals from a).

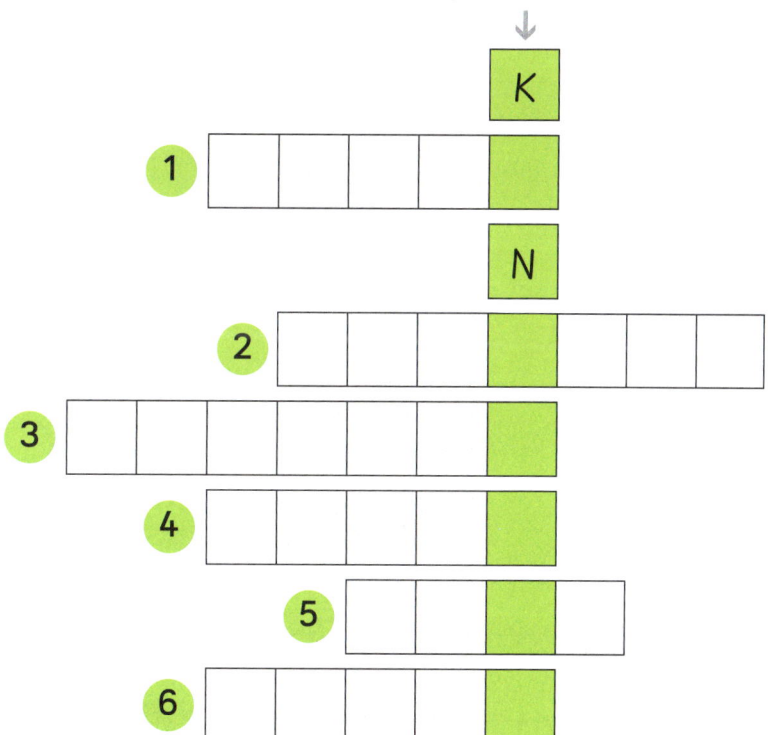

c) Write down the new word.

↓ _____

21 A tiger game

13/14
p. 44

Play the game with your partner.

Das Spiel findest du bei Aufgabe II im Anhang.

22 Your favourite animal

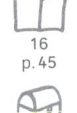
16
p. 45

Take notes about your favourite animal. Look at number 19 for help.

Schreibe hier nur Stichwörter auf, z. B. zu Größe, Farbe, Anzahl der Beine und Nahrung. Schlage neue Wörter im Wörterbuch nach.

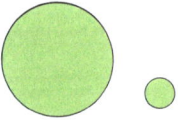

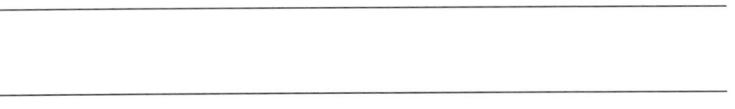

Wenn du ein Poster oder eine Präsentation vorbereitest, hilft es, wenn du zuerst Notizen machst. Dazu schreibst du keine ganzen Sätze, sondern nur Stichwörter auf.

23 An animal poster

16
p. 45

a) **Make a poster about <u>your</u> favourite animal.**
   Look at number 22 for help.

Du kannst das
Tier auch malen.

My favourite animals are _____.

They are _____.

They are _____.

They have got _____ legs.

They eat _____.

your favourite animal

b) **Present your poster in class.**

Complete the wordbank.

Sehenswürdigkeiten in London: (→ Seite 25–28)

– *Hyde Park* _____

_____

_____

_____

So sagst du, wie dir etwas gefällt: (→ Seite 29)

☺ _____

☹ _____

So sagst du, in welche Richtung jemand gehen soll: (→ Seite 30)

_____

_____

_____

Tiere im Zoo: (→ Seite 35)

_____ _____

_____ _____

_____ _____

Theme 3
Dreams

In diesem *Theme* ...

- lernst du, über die Zukunft und deine Zukunftsträume zu berichten.
- sprichst du über Berufe und Berufswünsche.
- beschäftigst du dich mit Robin Hood.

3 The future

1 Charlie's future

a) Look at the pictures.
   What can you see?

There's …   I can see …   There are …

2/3
p. 56/57

b) Listen and point.

23

 c) Match the pictures and the sentences.

"You'll have a lot of cars."   "You'll be rich."

"You'll be a football star."   "You'll live in a big house."

"You'll have twelve children."

2   The future rap

4
p. 57

24

a) Listen and read along.

Tell me the future!
Tell me the future!
Tell me the future, please!

You will have,
you will have
a zoo in seven years.

Tell me the future!
Tell me the future!
Tell me the future, please!

You will be,
you will be
a pop star in fifteen years.

Tell me the future!
Tell me the future!
Tell me the future, please!

You will live,
you will live
in a palace in twenty years.

b) Listen again and speak along.

Ihr könnt auch eine Strophe
zu euch selbst dichten.

So kannst du ausdrücken, dass etwas **in der Zukunft passieren wird**
(zum Beispiel morgen, nächste Woche oder nächstes Jahr):

I **will** be a football player.
You **will** live in London in twenty years.

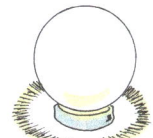

So kürzt du *will* ab: He**'ll** have a big house in ten years.

Achtung: *Will* nicht verwechseln mit dem deutschen „will" (= wollen).
    Das englische *I will* heißt auf Deutsch „ich werde".

3 Dream jobs?

Waiter ist ein Mann, *waitress* ist eine Frau.

5/7
p. 58/59

25

a) Listen and read along.

I love animals.
I think I'll be
a zoo-keeper.
1

I like cars.
I'll be
a car technician.
2

I like food.
I think I'll be
a cook.
3

I love plants.
I think I'll be
a gardener.
4

I like football.
I'll be
a football player.
5

I like people.
I think I'll be
a waitress.
6

 b) Match the sentences and the photos.

c) Talk to your partner.

Frage deine Lehrkraft, falls du
noch mehr Berufe wissen möchtest.

I love plants.
I think I'll be a gardener.
What about you?

I like …
I think I'll be a …

4   Tell me the future!

4
p.57

26

a)   **Listen. What is it about?**

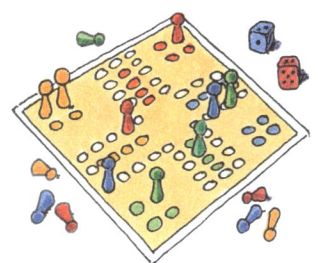

   b)   **Listen again and tick.**

1. Rajiv will be	a gardener	a pop star.
2. Karla will live	in New York	in London.
3. Rajiv will have	a zebra	a gorilla.

c)   **Now play the game with your partner.**

Tell me the future, please!

Das Spiel findest du bei
Aufgabe IV a) und b) im Anhang.

"You will have a sports car."

5 A word web

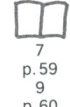

7
p. 59
9
p. 60

**Look at the words and the pictures.
Make a word web about your future.**

Du kannst deine Lehrkraft
nach weiteren Wörtern fragen.

In twenty years, I will be ...

_____

_____

_____

– happy
– rich
– a football player
– a gardener
– ...

my future

In twenty years, I will live ...

_____

_____

_____

In twenty years, I will have ...

_____

_____

_____

– in a big house
– in New York
– in Hamburg
– ...

Hamburg

– a big family
– two children
– a dog
– a car
– ...

6 Future cards

a) Write your future card. Look at number 5 for help.

9
p. 60

My future card

In twenty years,

I will be _____

_____ .

I will live _____ .

I will have _____

_____ .

b) Write a future card for a friend.

Wähle *he* oder *she*. Streiche das andere Wort einfach durch.

_____ 's future card

In twenty years,

he/she will _____

_____ .

He/She will _____ .

He/She will _____

_____ .

c) Present your future cards in class.

This is my future card.
In twenty years, I'll …

This is Cem's future card.
In twenty years, he'll …

7 **Daydreams**

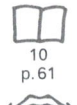
10
p.61

a) Look at the pictures.
What can you see?

b) Listen and read along.
27

Rajiv often dreams about his future.

Hockey is great.
I think I'll be a famous
hockey player.
I'll be rich then.

I like to help people.
I'll be a hero like Robin Hood.
Everyone will know me.

I love animals.
In some years, I'll have a tiger.
That'll be cool!

I want to have a big house.
I think I'll live
in Buckingham Palace.
We can have big parties then!

 c) Match the pictures and the sentences.

8 Robin Hood

11
p. 62–63

28

a) Listen and read along.

 b) What do you know about Robin Hood?
Talk about it in German.

Kennst du Robin Hood? Es gibt Lieder, Romane und Filme über ihn.
Robin Hood soll tatsächlich gelebt haben. Sein richtiger Name war wohl
Robert Earl of Huntington. Der Sage nach lebte er vor über 900 Jahren in
England. Robin Hood setzte sich für die Armen ein. Zusammen mit einer Gruppe
von Freunden lebte er versteckt im Wald, im Sherwood Forest bei Nottingham.
Man erkannte sie an ihren grünen Jacken und ihren Pfeilen und Bogen.
Robin Hoods größte Gegner waren Prinz John und der bösartige
Sheriff von Nottingham. Sie nahmen den Menschen ihr Land und ihr Geld weg.
Robin Hood und seine Freunde wollten den Verrätern das Geld wieder
abnehmen und es den Armen zurückgeben.
Deshalb wird Robin Hood oft als Held bezeichnet.

Wer ist für dich ein Held oder eine Heldin?

Ein Rollenspiel vorzuspielen macht viel Spaß!
Hier ein paar Tipps dazu:

- Verteilt zuerst die Rollen und legt fest, wer was sagt.
- Hört euch dann das Beispiel auf der CD an.
- Fragt eure Lehrkraft, falls ihr nicht wisst, wie man ein Wort ausspricht.
- Lernt den Dialog am besten in Abschnitten.
- Übt ihn mehrmals gemeinsam.
- Und: Denkt daran, laut und deutlich zu sprechen,
  wenn ihr das Rollenspiel vortragt.

9 Robin's story

13/15
p. 64/65

a) **Work with your partner.**
   Read out the sentences.

Versucht mal, die Sätze
unterschiedlich zu sprechen,
z. B. wütend, glücklich, traurig …

Help! Help!
The Sheriff has got my money!

I'm Robin Hood!
I'll get your money back!

We love
Robin Hood!

b) **Now look at number 8 again.**
   Act out the story in class.

Complete the wordbank.

So sprichst du über deine Zukunft: (→ Seite 46–51)

_____

_____

_____

So sprichst du über Berufswünsche: (→ Seite 48)

_____

_____

Berufe: (→ Seite 48)

– waiter / waitress _____

_____

_____

_____

_____

Dieses Wort konntest du dir schwer merken:

_____

Celebrations

In diesem *Theme* ...

- sprichst du über Feste und Feiern.
- erfährst du etwas über traditionelle Feste und Feste anderer Kulturen in Großbritannien.
- schreibst du über deinen Lieblingsfeiertag.
- sprichst du über Geburtstagsgeschenke.

1 Festivals

1
p. 80

29

a) Listen and point.

1 Christmas

2 Easter

3 Halloween

4 Chinese New Year

5 Eid

b) Match the pictures and the sentences.

It is New Year for Chinese people.

Children wear costumes and go from house to house.

Children often look for Easter eggs and chocolate.

It is a festival in winter, in December.

It is a festival for Muslims.

30

c) Listen and check.

2 A radio show

a) Listen. What is it about?

| animals | festivals | books |

b) Read the sentences. Then listen again and tick.

1. "My favourite
   festival is   Easter   Christmas."

2. "We always eat   apple cake   sausages."

3. "I get some great   presents   books."

4. "My favourite
   festival is   Eid   Halloween."

5. "We often have blue   orange juice   milk."

6. "We wear cool   T-shirts   costumes."

c) Talk to your classmates.

What's your
favourite festival?

I like Christmas best.
What about you?

My favourite festival
is Eid.

So kannst du über **dich und andere Personen** sprechen:

We wear cool costumes.
We eat sausages.
We have orange juice.

 **Land und Leute**

Die Briten haben ähnliche Feiertage wie wir. Die meisten feiern zum Beispiel Ostern (*Easter*) und Weihnachten (*Christmas*). Allerdings wird Weihnachten erst am 25. Dezember gefeiert – die Geschenke gibt es morgens!

Auch der Valentinstag (*Valentine's Day*), Muttertag (*Mother's Day*) und Halloween werden in Großbritannien gefeiert, teilweise schon viel länger als in Deutschland. Zum Valentinstag verschicken viele Menschen Karten.

Zur *Bonfire Night* im November zünden die Briten traditionell große Feuerwerke. Zu Silvester dagegen wird auf der Straße weniger Feuerwerk gezündet als in Deutschland.

Inzwischen werden in Großbritannien auch viele Feste anderer Kulturen gefeiert. Jedes Jahr gibt es eine große Parade zum Chinesischen Neujahr (*Chinese New Year*) in London. Das sogenannte Zuckerfest (*Eid*) markiert das Ende der muslimischen Fastenzeit (*Ramadan*).

Welche Feiertage feiert ihr in deiner Familie?

3 Let's celebrate

2
p. 81

33

Listen and number (1–5).

    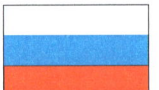

German   English   Chinese   Turkish   Russian

> Oft gibt es Bilder zu Texten. Sieh dir vor dem Lesen die Bilder an, um zu schauen, worum es geht. Dann verstehst du den Text viel leichter.

4 At the Chinese New Year parade

3/4
p.82/83

34

a) Look at the pictures.

b) Listen and point at the pictures.

Überlege zuerst, in welcher Reihenfolge die Geschichte ablaufen könnte.

> Rajiv and Charlie meet at 10 am.
> They want to go to Chinatown. **1**

> In Chinatown, there is a Chinese New Year parade. There are a lot of people there! **2**

> Rajiv and Charlie see a dragon! **3**

> At 1 pm, they have a snack. Mmmmm! **4**

> At 6 pm, they watch the Chinese New Year fireworks. **5**

 c) Read the texts. Match the pictures and the sentences.

birthday

wedding

Christmas

Mother's Day

Valentine's Day

5 A game

p. 84/85

Look at the photos on page 62.
Play the game with three or four classmates.

Das Spielfeld findest du
bei Aufgabe III im Anhang.

1
Count the people in
the birthday photo.

2
What is your favourite festival?

3
When is Christmas?

4
Go back to number 2.

5
Which of the festivals in the photos
do <u>you</u> celebrate?

6
Close your book.
Name two festivals.

7
Go back to number 5.

8 The English word for "Hochzeit"

is _____.

9
What do you do at Halloween?

10
What do you eat at Christmas?

11
When is Valentine's Day?

12
Go to number 15.

13
Find the birthday cake.

14
Go back to number 7.

15
Name a good birthday present for
your father.

16
The German word for
"Mother's Day"
is _____.

17
When is your birthday?

18
Go back to number 16.

19
When is Halloween?

20
The German word for
"Christmas"
is _____.

6 A word list

a) Find the German words in the list.
Write down the English words.

8/9
p. 86

vorbereiten: *prepare*

schmücken: _____

Rezept: _____

Karneval: _____

b) Complete the list
with the word pairs.

Neujahr – New Year

Musik – music

Mitternacht – midnight

German	English
K	
Karneval	carnival
Kuchen	cake
L	
Laterne	lantern
Lied	song
M	
Moschee	mosque

German	English
N	
O	
Ostern	Easter
P	
Party	party
Q	
Quiz	quiz
R	
Raketen	fireworks
Rezept	recipe
S	
schmücken	decorate
Schokolade	chocolate
T	
trinken	drink
U	
Überraschung	surprise
V	
Valentinstag	Valentine's Day
verkleiden	dress up
vorbereiten	prepare

Manchmal möchtest du etwas auf Englisch sagen, kennst aber das englische Wort nicht. Dann kannst du es in einer Wortliste oder einem Wörterbuch suchen. Sieh dir dabei auch den zweiten Buchstaben des Wortes an. Er zeigt dir, wo das Wort in der Liste steht.

Hier ist ein Beispiel:
„**Ra**keten" steht in der Liste vor „**Re**zept",
da „**a**" im Alphabet vor „**e**" kommt.

Raketen – fireworks
Raum – room
Rezept – recipe

7 A word web

8/9
p. 86

**Look at the words and the pictures.
Make a word web about your favourite festival.**

Du kannst auch ein Wörterbuch benutzen. Alle Jahreszeiten und Monate findest du auf Seite 126.

When it is: _____

– January   – winter
– February   – summer
– March   – …
– …

my favourite festival:

_____

What we eat and drink:

_____

_____

– sausages
– cake
– orange juice
– …

What we do:

_____

_____

– wear costumes
– have a party
– get some presents
– …

8 Your favourite festival

8/9
p.86

a) **Make a poster about your favourite festival.**
   Look at number 6 and 7 for help.

My favourite festival is

_____ .

It is in

_____ .

3
December

We always have

_____

_____

_____

_____ .

We often

_____

_____

_____

_____

_____ .

b) **Present your poster in class.**

9 Odd one out

Tick the odd one out.

10
p.87

1.	Caroline	Charlie	Easter	George
2.	Christmas	Halloween	Sunday	Eid
3.	present	music	cake	school
4.	lemonade	pizza	hamburger	cake

10 A chat

11/12
p.87

a) Read the chat. What is it about?

food and drink   a party   presents

Gilli@n: Hi Caroline!

Coco12:   Hi Gill! It's my mum's birthday soon.

Gilli@n: Cool! What will you buy for her?

Coco12:   I don't know. She likes books. She likes music, too.

Gilli@n: You can buy a CD then.

Coco12:   Yes. Or some chocolate. Or a nice birthday card.

Gilli@n: You can go to Oxford Street and buy a present there.

Coco12:   Good idea!

b) Read again. Underline the ideas for presents. un

11 Lots of presents

13
p.88

Look at the pictures.
Write down the words.

book • card • cake • CD

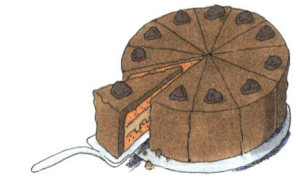

1 _____   2 _____

3 _____   4 _____

12 Birthday presents

13
p.88

a) **You want to find a present for your mum's birthday. Write down five ideas.**

Du kannst auch ein Wörterbuch benutzen.

_____

_____

_____

_____

_____

_____

b) **Talk to your partner.**

A book is a good present for my mum.

My mum likes …

Du kannst deine Liste in a) weiter ergänzen.

13 A special birthday

16/17
p. 89/90

35

a) Look at the pictures. What can you see?

There's … / There are …

b) Listen and read along.

I can see …

It's Mum's birthday soon.

Wow! I like this birthday card for Mum!

Hi Charlie! Let's bake a birthday cake for my mother.

There's chocolate and three eggs … oops … two eggs …

Happy birthday, Mum!

Let's eat the birthday cake.

 c) Is it true or false?

true   false

1. Caroline's mother's birthday is in summer.

2. Caroline buys a book for her mother.

3. They want to bake a cake.

4. They have got bananas and eggs.

5. They have a Christmas cake.

14 A birthday song

18
p. 91

36

a) Listen and sing along.

Happy birthday to you!

Happy birthday to you!

Happy birthday, dear Karla!

Happy birthday to you!

b) Talk to your partner.

> Which music style do you like best?

der erste = the first
der zweite = the second
der dritte = the third

> I like the first / second / third music style best. What about you?

15 A word search

19
p. 91

Find the words.

Du kannst sechs Wörter finden.

1	P	O	L	B	I	R	T	H	D	A	Y
2	C	A	K	E	V	O	J	W	Q	S	I
3	O	K	P	R	E	S	E	N	T	D	E
4	B	M	L	A	M	U	S	I	C	Z	N
5	X	T	E	C	R	I	C	A	R	D	P
6	Y	G	F	I	B	O	O	K	B	L	E

16 **Birthday words**

19
p. 91

a) Write down birthday words.

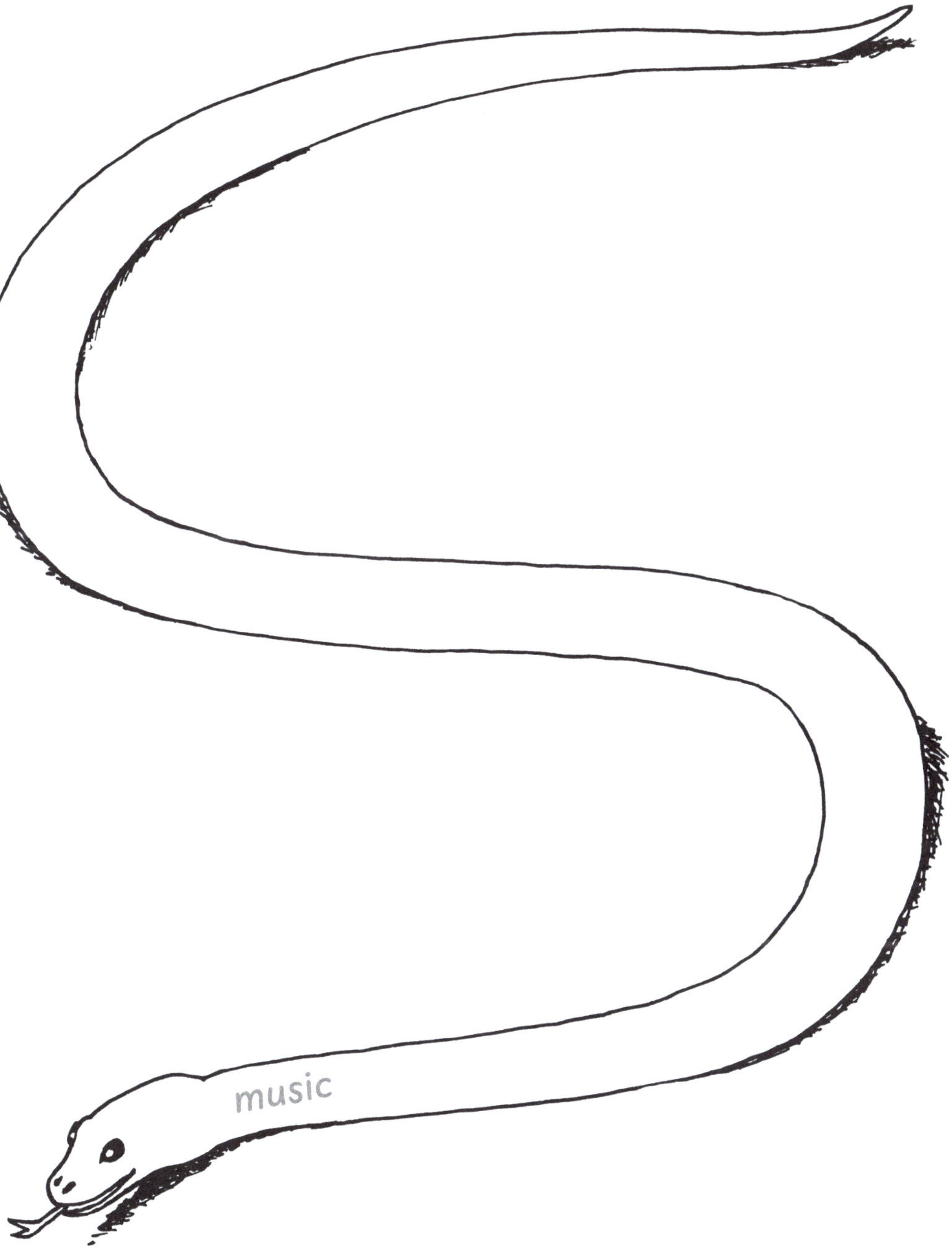

music

 b) Let your partner find the words.

Complete the wordbank.

Feste und Feiertage: (→ Seite 58, 62)

_____

_____

_____

_____

_____

Das wird an Feiertagen oft gemacht: (→ Seite 59)

_– We wear costumes._____

_____

_____

_____

Dinge, die man verschenken kann: (→ Seite 67, 68)

_____   _____

_____   _____

_____   _____

Theme 5

Dos and don'ts

In diesem *Theme* ...

- beschäftigst du dich mit Regeln daheim und in der Schule.
- berichtest du, was du zu Hause tun musst.
- beschreibst du, wie du etwas findest.
- erfährst du mehr über Schulregeln und Schuluniformen in Großbritannien.

1 Problems

a) Listen and point.

1/2
p. 102

37

 1

 2

 3

 4

 5

 6

b) Match the pictures and the sentences.

"Turn off your music!"   "Do your homework now!"

"Don't play football here!"   "Go to bed now!"

"Don't come home late!"   "Put on a clean T-shirt!"

c) Talk about the rules at your house.

My mum **always says**
"Don't come home late".

My ... often
says "...".

My brother **never says** "...".

always
often
1
2
3
never

2 Freeze!

1/2
p. 102

a) Act out one of the scenes in number 1. Then freeze. Let your classmates guess.

Ihr könnt die Szenen auch ohne Sprechen nachspielen.

That's picture number …

b) Act out the scene again and speak.

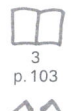

3 Karla

3
p. 103

a) Read the text and tick.

Weißt du noch?
I have to … = Ich muss …

Karla is   happy.   angry.   sad.

Saturday, 3 pm

Oh, I'm so angry! I want to meet Charlie in the park,

but I have to babysit my brother. I ALWAYS have to babysit

my brother. It's not fair! And I have to go to bed at 9:30 pm.

Why?? It's Saturday, and I'm not a baby …

 b) Why is Karla angry? Tick two answers.

She has to babysit her brother.

She has to go to the park.

She has to go to bed at 9:30 pm.

4 Go to bed now!

a) **Listen and repeat.**

Versuche einmal, den Satz genauso wütend, traurig oder fröhlich wie der Sprecher zu sagen. Es kann ruhig übertrieben sein.

p. 102–104

38

"Go to bed now!"

b) **Listen again and tick.**

1. angry   happy   sad

2. angry   happy   sad

3. angry   happy   sad

5 Your rules at home

a) **Write about the rules at <u>your</u> home.
Look at the box for help.**

5
p. 104

do my homework • babysit my brother •
tidy up my room • go to bed at 10 pm •
make my bed • turn off my music • …

1. I always have to _____

_____

2. I often have to _____

_____

3. I never have to _____

_____

 b) **Read out your sentences to your partner.**

6 Your top three list

7
p. 105

a) Read the list. What do you think:
Are the sports really boring?

boring sports

– tennis

– golf

– volleyball

Yes, I think … is boring.

No, I don't think … is boring.

b) Choose a word and a picture.
Then write your top three list.

boring   interesting   great   cool

 books

 singers

 computer games

 subjects

7 A poster

9
p. 106

a) Make a poster. Write down three rules for your family.

Du kannst dir auch eigene Regeln ausdenken. Male Bilder dazu.

Don't eat my chocolate! • **Turn off** the computer! •
Do my homework! • **Go** shopping every day! •
Put on cool clothes! • **Tidy up** my room! • ...

 b) Present your poster to your classmates.

8 Haverstock school rules

10
p. 107

39

a) Listen and point.

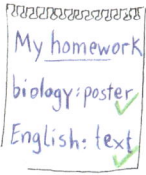

Be polite!

b) Listen again and read along.

Es sind nicht alle
Sätze aus dem
Hörtext abgedruckt.

HAVERSTOCK
SCHOOL RULES

1 Please be polite!

2 Don't be late!

3 Wear your school uniform!

4 Wear your sports clothes!

5 Don't eat in class!

6 Don't use your mobile phone!

7 Please do your homework!

c) Match the rules and the pictures.

d) Talk to your partner.

I think rule number …
is important.

I think rule number … is not important.

9 Oh no!

a) **Write the correct rules under the pictures. Look at number 8 for help.**

11
p. 108

Überlege dir, gegen welche Regel die Kinder verstoßen. Eine Regel bleibt übrig.

1

2

_____

_____

3

4

_____

_____

5

6

_____

_____

b) **Compare with your partner.**

Picture number … is
"Don't be late!"

c) **Look at a) again. Tick the rules at <u>your</u> school. Then read them out.**

Du kannst helfen, wenn jemand etwas auf Englisch nicht versteht,
wie zum Beispiel ein Schild. Denke daran, dass du dabei nicht Wort für Wort
übersetzen musst. Auf den Sinn kommt es an! Oft können dir auch Bilder
auf den Schildern helfen.

10 School signs

10/11
p. 107/108

Look at the signs. Explain them in German.

Land und Leute

An den meisten britischen Schulen tragen die Schülerinnen und Schüler eine
Schuluniform. Die Mädchen tragen oft einen Rock und eine Bluse mit Krawatte.
Die Jungen tragen meist eine Stoffhose und ein Hemd mit Krawatte.
Sportschuhe darf man dazu nicht tragen.

An der Schuluniform kann man direkt erkennen, auf welche Schule
jemand geht. Es gibt auch keinen Streit über die „richtige" Jeansmarke
oder das coolste Sweatshirt.

Fallen dir noch mehr Vor- und Nachteile einer Schuluniform ein?

11 Charlie's school uniform

Read the text.
What is Charlie's school uniform? Tick the correct picture.

Charlie always wears his school uniform to school.
He always wears black shoes.
Charlie never wears a T-shirt, jeans or shorts.
He always wears a blue blazer and black trousers.

12 Clothes

Match the pictures and the words.

shoes	shorts	T-shirt	cap
dress	trousers	pullover	skirt

13 What to wear?

12
p. 108

Talk to your classmates. What do <u>you</u> wear to school?

a T-shirt • a dress • jeans • a skirt • a sweatshirt •
shoes • a pullover • a bikini • shorts •
a blazer • a cap • flip-flops • trousers • …

I always wear jeans and
a T-shirt to school.

I often wear a pullover to school.

I never wear a dress to school.

14 What pupils say

13
p. 109

40

a) Listen and read along.

Hi, I'm Hannah. I'm 15 years old, and I live
in Bristol. I don't like my school uniform.
It's black and white.
I want to wear my own clothes!

Hi, my name is Joel. I'm 13 years old.
I live in Milton Keynes.
I think my school uniform is cool.
We'll have a new logo soon. It'll be great.

b) Talk to your classmates.

| Would you like to wear a school uniform? | Yes. I think it's cool. | No. I think it's boring. |

15 At the bus stop

a) Read the sentences. Match
the sentences and the people.

Eine Sprechblase bleibt übrig.

1 OK, OK. I'll give you my money.
But please don't hit me.

2 Can you give me
your money, please?

3 Give me your money!

b) Look at the picture in a) again.
Talk about it in German.

Hast du schon einmal ähnliche
Situationen beobachtet?
Was könnten die anderen
Personen auf dem Bild tun?

16 Let's be polite

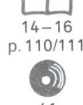

a) Listen and read along.

14–16
p. 110/111

41

Rule number one is to be polite.
Then everyone always feels alright.

We say "Hello!" to people at school.
We say "Sorry!" or "Please!", and that's cool.

Let's say "Hi!" when we meet someone new,
"Nice to meet you!" or "How are you?"

Ihr könnt auch im Team arbeiten.
Jeder kann eine Strophe lernen.

b) Learn the poem.
Present it in class.

Wenn du ein Wort auf Englisch nicht weißt, frage deine Lehrkraft:

What's the English word for Krawatte? – That's a "tie".

17 **My dream school uniform**

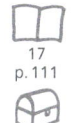

17
p. 111

a) **Draw your dream school uniform. Label it.**

Du kannst deine Mitschüler oder deine Lehrkraft nach neuen Wörtern fragen.

 b) **Present your poster in class.**

Complete the wordbank.

Einige Regeln an der Schule und zu Hause: (→ Seite 74, 79)

— *Turn off your music!*

_____

_____

_____

_____

Wörter, die beschreiben, wie etwas oder jemand ist: (→ Seite 76, 77)

— *boring*

_____

_____

Kleidungsstücke: (→ Seite 82, 83)

— *shoes*

_____

_____

_____

Theme 6

Let's go!

In diesem *Theme* ...

- erzählst du, was du am Wochenende vorhast.
- lernst du, jemandem gute Besserung zu wünschen.
- sprichst du über Fersehsendungen.
- lernst du Urlaubs- und Freizeitaktivitäten in Großbritannien kennen.
- berichtest du über deine Urlaubspläne.

6 What's on?

1 Weekend activities

a) **Work with your partner.**
Guess the activities.

Wenn du Wörter nicht mehr weißt,
kannst du auch erst Aufgabe b) lösen.

What's activity number ...?

I think it's watching TV.

1

2

3

4

5

6

b) **Find the activities.**

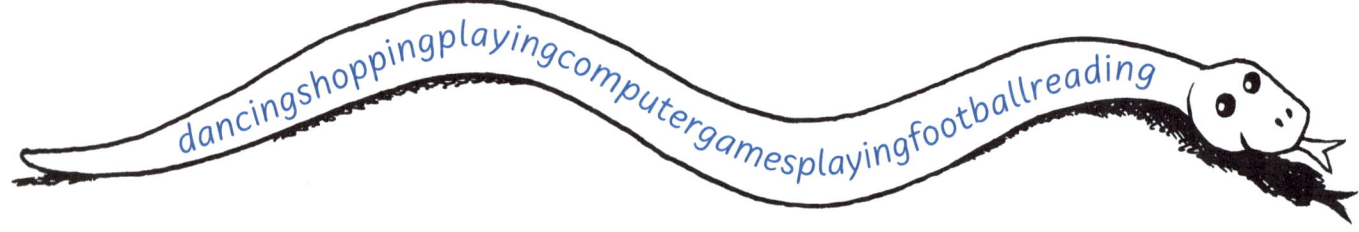

dancingshoppingplayingcomputergamesplayingfootballreading

listeningtomusicmeetingfriendswatchingTVplayingtennis

2  **Gillian and Karla**

 a) Listen. What is it about?

holiday plans   a birthday party   weekend plans

b) Listen again and tick.

"Let's listen to music."

"Let's play basketball."

"Let's go to the park."

"Let's play computer games."

c) What do they decide? Tick two answers.

d) Tick the correct box.

They want to meet on Saturday at …

two o'clock.   two thirty.   four o'clock.

3 A weekend in Camden

a) Read the texts.

2/3
p. 122/123

Charlie (11:15):

Hi Karla!

I'm ill – and I'm in bed.

I think I'll just watch TV and listen to music this weekend. And I want to play computer games.

What are your plans for the weekend?

C.

Karla (11:30):

Hi Charlie!

On Saturday I want to meet Gillian in the park. I think I'll watch a music show on TV on Sunday.

Get well soon!!

K.

b) Is it true or false?

true   false

1. Charlie is ill.

2. Charlie is at school.

3. Charlie wants to listen to music.

4. Karla wants to meet Gillian in the park.

5. Karla wants to sing in a music show.

c) Ask your partner.

What are your plans for the weekend?

I want to … / I think I'll …

go to the park • meet friends •
play football • watch TV •
play computer games •
go shopping • read a book •
listen to music • dance •
go inline skating • …

4 A get well card

a) Read the cards.

Hi Alex,

Get well soon!

Love,

Jacky

Hi Sevda,

We miss you at school!

Love,

Ben

b) Write a get well card for a good friend.

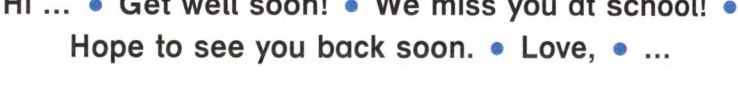

Hi ... • Get well soon! • We miss you at school! •
Hope to see you back soon. • Love, • ...

Land und Leute

Wie bei uns gibt es auch in Großbritannien ein großes Angebot an Fernsehsendern. Bekannt sind vor allem die Fernsehsender *BBC1* und *BBC2*.

Mit Begeisterung schauen viele Jugendliche in Großbritannien Talentshows, die auf verschiedenen Sendern gezeigt werden. Bei den Sendungen *X-Factor* und *The Voice* werden die besten Sänger gesucht. *Britain's Got Talent* zeigt alles von tanzenden Hunden bis hin zu Feuerspuckern.

Welche deutschen Shows dieser Art kennst du?

5 TV programmes

Charlie is ill. He wants to watch TV.

7
p. 125

43

a) Listen and point.

1
_____

2
_____

3
_____

4
_____

5
_____

6
_____

b) Listen again and tick.

Charlie wants to watch   the news.   the music show.

c) Label the photos in a).
Then check with your partner.

a music show • a quiz show • a film •
the news • a cartoon • a sports programme

d) Talk to your classmates.

I often watch a film on TV.

I always watch … on TV.

I never watch … on TV.

6 Your weekend

a) **Make a poster about <u>your</u> weekend.**
   Look at the pictures and number 3 c) for help.

Du kannst die Uhren
selbst ausfüllen.

My weekend

This weekend, I want to get up at

_____.

I think I will have breakfast at _____.

At _____ , I will _____

_____.

Then I want to _____

_____.

I will go to bed at _____.

At the weekend, I always _____

_____.

I never _____.

7 **Holidays in Britain**

a) **Read the flyer. What is it about?**

Du kannst dir die Informationen auch auf CD anhören.
44

a football camp   a football club

FOOTBALL CAMP – for kids from 6 to 16

Do you like football?
Then come to our summer camp
in Manchester!

You will have training every day.

Every evening there are activities
like discos and karaoke nights.
You can also come to our
quiz nights. Or you can just
listen to music and watch TV.

b) **Read again. Tick the correct words.**

1. The camp is for kids from   5 to 14   6 to 16 years.

2. It is in   London   Manchester.

3. There is training every   day   week.

c) **Talk to your partner in German.**
   What else do you understand?

8 **The kids' holidays**

13
p. 128

a) **Read the dialogue. What is it about?**

holiday clubs

holiday plans

Caroline: School will be over soon.

Charlie: Yes, that'll be great.

Caroline: We want to go to Greece. What about you, Charlie?

Charlie: I think I'll go to a football camp in Manchester.

Caroline: Wow, that's cool! What about you, Nick?

Nick: We want to go to Scotland.

b) **Talk to your classmates.**

What are your plans
for the holidays?

I want to go to …

I think I'll play …

We want to go to …

Wenn ihr auf Englisch miteinander sprecht, achtet darauf,
deutlich zu sprechen. Es ist nicht schlimm, wenn ihr euch versprecht
oder Fehler macht. Nehmt euch Zeit und setzt euch nicht unter Druck.
Dann klappt es mit dem Sprechen viel besser.

9 The dog in the fog

Überlege einmal, wovon die Geschichte handeln könnte.

a) Look at the pictures. What can you see?

15
p. 129

It is the summer holidays. David, his parents and his dog Kenny are in Wales. They want to climb Mount Snowdon.

Oh, no! There's so much fog.

But where is the dog?

There was a dog.
He helped us find the way.

b) Read the sentences. Match the sentences and the pictures.

1 Look, there's a big dog!

2 That was Gerret, the dog. He lives in the mountains.

3 I can't see anything.

4 Great, we're back.

5 Let's climb the mountain!

45

c) Listen and check.

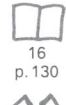

10 The trip

16
p.130

Look at number 9 again.
Circle the correct words.

1. David, his   parents   /   friends   and his dog are on holiday.

2. They are in   Scotland   /   Wales .

3. There is much   fog   /   food .

4. A   dog   /   cat   helps them.

5. The dog's name is   Gelert   /   Gerret .

11 Kenny's story

18
p.130

a) Look at number 9 again.
    Then read the sentences. Find the correct order.

He helped us find the way.

He lives in the mountains.

Then there was a big black dog.

It was Gerret, the dog.

David, his parents and I wanted to climb Mount Snowdon.

There was much fog.

   b) Check with your partner.

12  **Your holiday plans**

a) **Make a collage about <u>your</u> holiday plans.**

19
p. 131

Du kannst ein Wörterbuch benutzen.

go swimming • meet my friends •
go inline skating • go to Paris •
eat ice cream • play computer games • ...

_____

_____

_____

_____

_____

_____

 b) **Present your poster in class.**   In my holidays I want to ...

13 A game

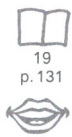

19
p.131

Play the game with three or four classmates.

Das Spielfeld findest du bei Aufgabe III im Anhang.

1
Look at page 89 again.
What colour is Gillian's T-shirt?

2
Count the dogs on page 96.

3
The English word for "Nachrichten"

is _____.

4
Find the football on page 94.

5
Name two activities for the weekend.

6
Name a TV programme.

7
Go back to number 4.

8
Name a quiz show.

9
Look at page 96 again.
Where are David and his
parents on holiday?

10
Go back to number 8.

11
What is "Get well soon!"
in German?

12
Look at page 89 again.
What is the name of David's dog?

13
Look at page 94 again.
Where is the football camp?

14
Go to number 17.

15
Count the pencils on page 97.

16
Look at page 96 again.
What colour is David's cap?

17
Look at page 92 again.
Which sport can you see
in the picture?

18
When do you get up
at the weekend?

19
Go back to number 13.

20
What is your favourite
TV show?

Complete the wordbank.

Dinge, die man am Wochenende machen kann: (→ Seite 88, 90)

– playing basketball

_____

_____

_____

So fragst du, was jemand am Wochenende vor hat: (→ Seite 90)

_____

Sätze, die man auf eine Karte schreiben kann: (→ Seite 91)

_____

_____

_____

Fernsehsendungen: (→ Seite 92)

_____

_____

_____

A The legend[1] of Gelert

"The legend of Gelert" is a legend about a prince[2] and his big black dog.

Llewellyn is a prince. He has got a baby
and a dog.
He is Llewellyn's best friend.
The baby's mother died[3].

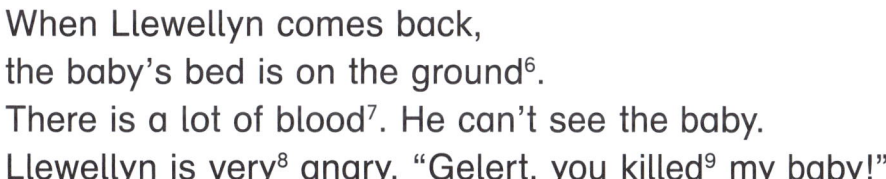

One day, Llewellyn goes out[4].
He leaves[5] the baby at home
with his dog Gelert.
He says to Gelert: "Watch the baby."

When Llewellyn comes back,
the baby's bed is on the ground[6].
There is a lot of blood[7]. He can't see the baby.
Llewellyn is very[8] angry. "Gelert, you killed[9] my baby!"

Llewellyn is so angry that he kills Gelert. –
But what is that? The baby cries[10].
It is under the bed.
And then Llewellyn sees a big wolf.
It is dead[11].
The blood isn't from the baby.
It is from Gelert and the wolf!

"Oh no! Gelert didn't[12] kill my baby!
Gelert helped my baby. He killed the wolf!"
says Llewellyn. "I've killed my best friend!"

Llewellyn is very sad about Gelert.

Sucht im Internet
ein Bild von Gelerts
Grab *Beddgelert*.

He makes a big grave[13] for Gelert. The grave is still[14] in Wales.
Its[15] name is Beddgelert – Gelert's grave.

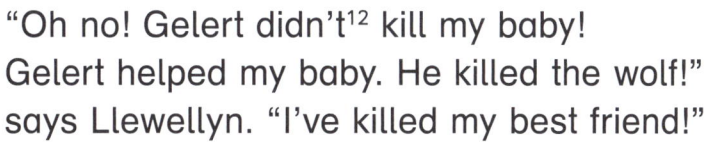

[1] legend – Legende	[6] ground – (Erd)boden	[11] dead – tot
[2] prince – Prinz	[7] blood – Blut	[12] didn't – tat nicht
[3] died – starb	[8] very – sehr	[13] grave – Grab
[4] goes out – geht aus / geht weg	[9] killed – hast … getötet	[14] still – immer noch
[5] leaves – hier: lässt … zu Hause	[10] cries – weint	[15] its – sein

B   A horoscope[1]

D
p. 145

47

Versuche doch einmal zu raten,
wie die Sternzeichen auf Deutsch heißen.

Aries
(21 March – 19 April)

Don't buy
too much
this month!

Taurus
(20 April – 20 May)

Be[2] nice and
someone
will be nice
to you.

Gemini
(21 May – 20 June)

This month you
will meet
someone new.

Cancer
(21 June – 22 July)

You are happy
when you
are with
your friends.

Leo
(23 July – 22 August)

Listen to your
heart[3].
It will tell you
what to do.

Virgo
(23 August – 22 Sept.)

You will go to
a party!

Libra
(23 Sept. – 22 Oct.)

Always say
what you think.
But be careful[4]
this month.

Scorpio
(23 Oct. – 21 Nov.)

This is a good
month for you.
You will get
a present.

Sagittarius
(22 Nov. – 21 Dec.)

You will have a
great weekend.

Capricorn
(22 Dec. – 19 Jan.)

You will make
a new friend[5]
next[6] week.

Aquarius
(20 Jan. – 18 Feb.)

A classmate
is sad.
Make him or
her happy.

Pisces
(19 Feb. – 20 March)

It is boring
today.
It will get
better[7] soon.

---

[1] horoscope – Horoskop
[2] Be … – Sei …
[3] heart – Herz
[4] careful – vorsichtig

[5] make a new friend – eine neue
   Freundschaft schließen
[6] next – nächste
[7] get better – besser werden

● Das muss ich noch üben.
● Das geht schon ganz gut.
● Das kann ich.

Liebe Schülerin, lieber Schüler,

auf den folgenden Seiten findest du sechs Portfolio-Fragebögen, zu jedem Themenabschnitt einen. Jedes Mal, wenn ihr einen Abschnitt fertig bearbeitet habt, füllst du einen Fragebogen aus. So kannst du feststellen, was du schon kannst.

Das geht so: Sieh dir z. B. den folgenden Satz an.
Überlege, wie gut du das kannst, was dort beschrieben ist:

○ **Ich kann Fragen zu den Ferien stellen und beantworten.**
(→ Seite 9, 10)

Vor jedem Satz steht ein Kreis: ○
Darunter steht die Seite,
auf der es eine Aufgabe dazu gibt:
(→ Seite 9, 10)

Wenn du meinst, dass du das Beschriebene
schon richtig gut kannst,
dann male den Kreis grün aus: ●

Du bist dir noch nicht ganz sicher?
Dann male den Kreis gelb aus: ●

Wenn du noch große Schwierigkeiten hast,
dann male den Kreis rot aus: ●

Und jetzt: Viel Spaß!

1 After the holidays

Holidays

○ Ich kann ein Gespräch verstehen und
die Sätze in die richtige Reihenfolge bringen.
(→ Seite 9)

○ Ich kann Fragen zu den Ferien stellen und beantworten.
(→ Seite 9, 10)

○ Ich kann Wörter zu meinen Ferien in einem Wortnetz
sammeln und dann über die Ferien berichten.
(→ Seite 13)

○ Ich kann eine Postkarte aus dem Urlaub
lesen und selbst eine schreiben.
(→ Seite 14)

Back to school

○ Ich kann ein Gespräch führen, um jemanden kennenzulernen.
(→ Seite 18, 19)

○ Ich kann mithilfe eines Wortnetzes ein Poster
über meine Schule erstellen und präsentieren.
(→ Seite 20, 21)

○ Ich kann eine Website lesen und verstehen.
(→ Seite 16)

○ Ich kenne verschiedene Schulfächer auf Englisch.
(→ Seite 15)

2 Around London

Famous sights

○ Ich kann bei einer Führung verstehen,
um welche Sehenswürdigkeiten es geht.
(→ Seite 26 – 28)

○ Ich kann eine Wegbeschreibung verstehen,
nach dem Weg fragen und einfache Wege beschreiben.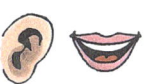
(→ Seite 30 – 32)

○ Ich kann mich darüber unterhalten,
wie mir Sehenswürdigkeiten gefallen.
(→ Seite 29)

○ Ich kann ein Poster über London erstellen.
(→ Seite 34)

London Zoo

○ Ich kann verstehen, wann etwas gemacht wird.
(→ Seite 39)

○ Ich kenne einige Zootiere auf Englisch
und kann über sie sprechen.
(→ Seite 35, 40, 41)

○ Ich kann eine Präsentation zu meinem Lieblingstier
halten, die ich mit Notizen vorbereitet habe.
(→ Seite 42, 43)

○ Ich kann einen einfachen Comic lesen und verstehen.
(→ Seite 36)

3 Dreams

The future

○ Ich verstehe Gespräche über die Zukunft.
(→ Seite 46, 49)

○ Ich kann über die Zukunft und
meine Berufswünsche sprechen.
(→ Seite 48, 49)

○ Ich kenne einige Berufe auf Englisch.
(→ Seite 48)

○ Ich kann mithilfe von Notizen
einen kurzen Text über meine Zukunft schreiben.
(→ Seite 50, 51)

Heroes

○ Ich kann verstehen und mitlesen,
wenn jemand über Zukunftswünsche spricht.
(→ Seite 52)

○ Ich kann Sätze verschieden betont sprechen.
(→ Seite 55)

○ Ich kann ein einfaches Rollenspiel vorführen.
(→ Seite 55)

○ Ich kann einen einfachen Comic lesen und verstehen.
(→ Seite 53)

4 Celebrations

Festivals

○ **Ich kann verstehen, worum es in einer Radiosendung geht.**
(→ Seite 59)

○ **Ich kann sagen, wie ich bestimmte Feiertage finde.**
(→ Seite 59)

○ **Ich kann eine Geschichte mithilfe von Bildern verstehen.**
(→ Seite 61)

○ **Ich kann Wörter in einer deutsch-englischen Wortliste finden.**
(→ Seite 64)

Birthdays

○ **Ich kann Wörter zum Thema Geschenke sammeln und anschließend darüber sprechen.**
(→ Seite 68)

○ **Ich kann beschreiben, was ich auf Bildern sehe.**
(→ Seite 69)

○ **Ich kann einen Chat lesen und verstehen.**
(→ Seite 67)

○ **Ich kann ein Worträtsel mit Geburtstagswörtern erstellen.**
(→ Seite 71)

5 Dos and don'ts

Rules at home

◯ **Ich kann berichten,
welche Regeln es bei uns zu Hause gibt.**
(→ Seite 74, 76)

◯ **Ich kann einen Tagebucheintrag lesen und verstehen.**
(→ Seite 75)

◯ **Ich kann beschreiben, wie etwas ist.**
(→ Seite 77)

◯ **Ich kann Regeln für meine Familie aufschreiben.**
(→ Seite 78)

Rules at school

◯ **Ich kann Schulregeln verstehen und sie Bildern zuordnen.**
(→ Seite 79)

◯ **Ich kann ein Gedicht auswendig lernen und vortragen.**
(→ Seite 84)

◯ **Ich kann verschiedene Kleidungsstücke
benennen und sagen, was ich oft anziehe.**
(→ Seite 82, 83)

◯ **Ich kann auf Deutsch englische Schilder erklären.**
(→ Seite 81)

6 Let's go!

What's on?

○ Ich kann ein Gespräch über Wochenendpläne verstehen.
(→ Seite 89)

○ Ich kann über Wochenendpläne sprechen.
(→ Seite 90)

○ Ich kann einige Fernsehsendungen auf Englisch
benennen und sagen, wie oft ich sie schaue.
(→ Seite 92)

○ Ich kann ein Poster über mein Wochenende erstellen.
(→ Seite 93)

Holidays

○ Ich kann ein Gespräch über Urlaubspläne
verstehen und selbst eins führen.
(→ Seite 95)

○ Ich kann auf Deutsch über einen englischen Flyer sprechen.
(→ Seite 94)

○ Ich kann Bildern passende Sprechblasen zuordnen.
(→ Seite 96)

○ Ich kann eine Collage über meine Urlaubspläne erstellen.
(→ Seite 98)

Auf den folgenden Seiten kannst du noch einmal nachschlagen, wie du etwas sagen kannst.

1

So kannst du auf Englisch **über dich selbst** Auskunft geben:

My name is Emma.

I am ten (years old). / **I'm** ten (years old).

I have got a brother. / **I've got** a brother.

I haven't got a dog.

2

So sagst du, ob du etwas **magst**:

😊 I **like** chocolate.

☹ I **don't like** ice cream.

So **fragst** du, ob jemand etwas **mag**:

Do you **like** eggs for breakfast? — Yes, I do. / No, I don't.

So **fragst** du, was jemand **besonders gerne mag**:

What's your **favourite** colour?

3

So kannst du sagen, was du **gerne tun würdest**:

I'd like to see Madame Tussauds.

So kannst du ausdrücken, **wie** dir etwas **gefällt**:

☺ That's **great** / **interesting**.

☹ That's **boring**.

4

So sagst du, dass du etwas **tun musst**:

I **have to** tidy up my room.

5

So kannst du **über eine andere Person** Auskunft geben:

 His name is Max.

He is from England. /
He's from England.

He has got green eyes.

He has to tidy up his room.

 **Her** name is Elisa.

She is eleven years old. /
She's eleven years old.

She likes orange juice.

She wants to play tennis.

Weißt du noch? Bei einem **Tier** sagt man *it*:

It likes apples.

6

So kannst du über **dich und andere Personen** sprechen:

We wear cool costumes.
We eat sausages.
We have orange juice.

7

So kannst du über **mehrere Personen, Tiere** oder **Dinge** sprechen:

My favourite teachers **are** cool. / **They are** cool.

Tigers **eat** meat. / **They eat** meat.

Lions **have got** four legs. / **They have got** four legs.

8

So kannst du von **mehreren Dingen** oder **Personen** sprechen:

1 football → 2 football**s**

1 banana → 2 banana**s**

Pass auf:

1 hero → 2 hero**es**

9

So sagst du, **wem** (oder **zu wem**) etwas **gehört**:

It is Karla**'s** birthday.

10

So sagst du, **wie häufig** du etwas tust:

I **always** eat cake on my birthday.

I **often** wear jeans to school.

I **never** make my bed.

11

So kannst du ausdrücken, dass etwas **in der Zukunft passieren wird** (zum Beispiel morgen, nächste Woche oder nächstes Jahr):

I **will** be a football player.

You **will** live in London in twenty years.

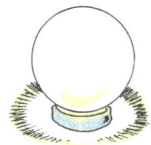

So kürzt du *will* ab: He'**ll** have a big house in ten years.

Achtung: *Will* nicht verwechseln mit dem deutschen „will" (= wollen). Das englische *I will* heißt auf Deutsch „ich werde".

12

So kannst du sagen, was schon **passiert ist** (zum Beispiel gestern, letzte Woche oder letztes Jahr):

I **had** ice cream every day.
It **was** rainy.
Karla **played** basketball.
Rajiv **went** to Camden Market.

Fragen stellst du so:

Where **was** Charlie?
What **did** you do?

13

So kannst du **Fragen stellen**:

What's your hobby?
When is your birthday?
Where are you from?
How old are you?

14

So kannst du beschreiben, **was es** (irgendwo) **gibt**:

There is a chair. / **There's** a chair.   **There are** two chairs.

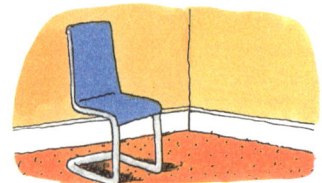   

15

So sagst du, **wo genau** sich etwas befindet:

The smiley is **on** the box.

The smiley is **in** the box.

The smiley is **under** the box.

16

So sagst du, **in welche Richtung** jemand gehen soll:

Turn left into Park Street.

Turn right into School Road.

Go straight on.

So **fragst** du nach dem Weg:

Excuse me, please. How can I get to the supermarket?

17

So sagst du, **an welchem Wochentag** etwas passiert:

The judo club is **on** Tuesday.

So sagst du, **in welchem Monat** etwas passiert:

My birthday is **in** June.

So fragst du, **wann** etwas ist:

When is your birthday?

18

So kannst du Wörter im Englischen **abkürzen**, wenn du sprichst oder z. B. eine E-Mail schreibst:

I **am** = I'**m**
I **have got** = I'**ve got**
I **will** = I'**ll**
I **would** = I'**d**

you **are** = you'**re**
they **are** = they'**re**

they **have got** = they'**ve got**

it **is** = it'**s**
what **is** = what'**s**
that **is** = that'**s**
there **is** = there'**s**

let **us** = let'**s**

A

a / an	ein(e)
about	über
activity	Aktivität
after	nach
again	wieder, noch einmal
alright	in Ordnung, gut
also	auch
always	immer
and	und
angry	wütend
animal	Tier
answer	Antwort; antworten
anything	(irgend)etwas
apple	Apfel
are	bist / sind / seid
around	um; herum
art	Kunst
at	in; an; um
autumn	Herbst

a postcard / an egg

1 **activity** – 2 activities

I **am** – ich bin
you **are** – du bist
he **is** / she **is** / it **is** – er ist / sie ist / es ist
we **are** – wir sind
you **are** – ihr seid
they **are** – sie sind

I **was** – ich war

around London – um London herum

B

babysit	babysitten
back	zurück
bake	backen
banana	Banane
be	sein
beach	Strand
bed	Bett
best	am liebsten, beste(r, s)
big	groß
biology	Biologie
birthday	Geburtstag
black	schwarz
blue	blau
book	Buch
boring	langweilig
boy	Junge
breakfast	Frühstück
bridge	Brücke
brother	Bruder
brown	braun
bus stop	Bushaltestelle
but	aber
buy	kaufen

I like ... **best**. – Ich mag ... am liebsten.

Happy **birthday!** – Herzlichen Glückwunsch zum Geburtstag!

have **breakfast** – frühstücken

C

cake	Kuchen
campsite	Campingplatz

can / can't	können / nicht können	
car	Auto	sports **car** – Sportwagen
car technician	Automechaniker(in)	
card	Karte	
castle	Burg; Schloss	
cat	Katze	
celebrate	feiern	
celebration	Feier, Fest	
chair	Stuhl	
child	Kind	1 **child** – 2 children
Chinese	Chinesisch; chinesisch	
chocolate	Schokolade	
Christmas	Weihnachten	
cinema	Kino	
city	Stadt	
class	Klasse; Unterricht	in **class** – in der Klasse
classmate	Mitschüler(in), Klassenkamerad(in)	
clean	sauber	
climb	(hinauf)klettern; (hinauf)steigen	
close	schließen	
clothes	Kleider, Kleidung	
colour	Farbe	
come	kommen	**Come** on! – Komm jetzt!, Mach schon!
computer game	Computerspiel	
cook	Koch / Köchin	
correct	richtig	
costume	Kostüm	
count	zählen	
cute	süß, niedlich	

D

dance	tanzen	
dancing	Tanzen	
dangerous	gefährlich	
day	Tag	
daydream	Tagtraum	
dear	liebe(r, s) (z. B. in Briefen)	
December	Dezember	
decide	entscheiden	
dialogue	Dialog	
dictionary	Wörterbuch	
did	tat(est, et)	What **did** you do? – Was hast du gemacht?
different	unterschiedlich	

do / don't	tun / nicht tun
dog	Hund
dragon	Drache
draw	zeichnen
dream	Traum; träumen
dress	Kleid
drink	trinken

Do you like ...? – Magst du ...?
Don't come home late! –
   Komm nicht zu spät nach Hause!

E

Easter	Ostern
eat	essen; bei Tieren: fressen
egg	Ei
Eid	Zuckerfest (muslimisches Fest am Ende der Fastenzeit)
what else	was noch, was sonst
end	Ende, Schluss
English	Englisch; englisch
evening	Abend
every	jede(n, r, s)
everyone	alle; jeder
Excuse me!	Entschuldigen Sie!

in the **end** – zum Schluss

F

false	falsch
family	Familie
famous	berühmt
fast	schnell
father	Vater
favourite	Lieblings-
February	Februar
feed	füttern
feel	(sich) fühlen
festival	Fest
find	finden
fireworks	Feuerwerk
first	erste(r, s); zuerst
fish	Fisch
focus	Fokus, Schwerpunkt
fog	Nebel
food	Essen
football	Fußball
for	für; um
freeze	erstarren
French	Französisch; französisch
friend	Freund(in)

What's your **favourite** ...? –
   Was ist dein Lieblings-...?

the **first** – der / die / das erste

1 **fish** – 2 fish

language in **focus** –
   Redemittelanhang bei *Camden Market*

for you – für dich
for help – um Hilfe

from	von; aus
funny	lustig, witzig
future	Zukunft

Where are you **from**? –
  Woher kommst du?
from the top – von ganz oben

G

game	Spiel
gardener	Gärtner(in)
geography	Erdkunde
German	Deutsch; deutsch
get	bekommen; kommen
get up	aufstehen
Get well soon!	Gute Besserung!
give	geben
go	gehen; fahren
goldfish	Goldfisch
good	gut
great	großartig, toll
Greece	Griechenland
green	grün

in **German** – auf Deutsch

get back – zurückbekommen; zurückholen

H

had	hatte(n); aß(en)
happy	glücklich
has	hat; isst; trinkt
has got	hat
has to	muss
have	haben; essen; trinken
have got	haben
have to	müssen
he	er
hello	hallo
help	Hilfe; helfen
her	ihr(e); sie
here	hier
hero	Held(in)
hippo	Nilpferd
his	sein(e)
history	Geschichte
hit	schlagen
holiday, holidays	Urlaub, Ferien
home	Zuhause; nach Hause
homework	Hausaufgaben
hope	hoffen
house	Haus; Zuhause
how	wie

I **have (got)** – ich habe
you **have (got)** – du hast
he / she / it **has (got)** –
  er / sie / es hat
we **have (got)** – wir haben
you **have (got)** – ihr habt
they **have (got)** – sie haben

I **have to** go to bed. –
  Ich muss ins Bett gehen.

for **help** – um Hilfe
I **helped** – ich half

Here you are! – Hier, bitte!, Bitte schön!

1 **hero** – 2 heroes

on **holiday** – im Urlaub

at **home** – zu Hause

How are you? – Wie geht es dir?
How can I get there? –
  Wie komme ich dorthin?

I

I	ich
ice cream	Eiscreme
ICT	Informatikunterricht
idea	Idee
ill	krank
important	wichtig
in	in, im; auf
India	Indien
inline skating	Inlineskaten
interesting	interessant
into	in (hinein)
is / isn't	ist / ist nicht
it	es

Turn left **into** Top Road. –
   Biege nach links in die Top Road ab.

he **is** / she **is** / it **is** – er ist / sie ist / es ist

J

January	Januar
June	Juni
just	nur; einfach

K

kangaroo	Känguru
know	kennen; wissen

L

language	Sprache
late	(zu) spät
left	links
leg	Bein
lemonade	Limonade
let	lassen
Let's …!	Lass(t) uns …!
library	Bibliothek, Bücherei
like	mögen; wie
lion	Löwe
list	Liste
listen	(zu)hören
listening	Zuhören; Hören
live	leben, wohnen
look for …	nach … suchen
lost	verloren
a lot of, lots of	viel(e)
love	lieben, sehr gern mögen; viele Grüße (z. B. in Briefen)
lunch	Mittagessen

language in focus –
   Redemittelanhang bei *Camden Market*

Turn **left**. – Biege links ab.

I (don't) **like** … – Ich mag … (nicht).
I'd **like** to … – Ich würde gerne …
like best – am liebsten mögen
He is **like** Robin Hood. –
   Er ist wie Robin Hood.

listen / **listening** to music – Musik hören

M

make	machen
man	Mann
many	viele
map	Karte
March	März
maths	Mathe
May	Mai
me	mir; mich
meat	Fleisch
meet	treffen, sich treffen
meeting	Treffen
milk	Milch
miss	vermissen
mobile phone	Handy
money	Geld
month	Monat
mother	Mutter
Mother's Day	Muttertag
mountain	Berg
Mr (= Mister)	Herr (in der Anrede)
Mrs	Frau (in der Anrede)
much	viel
mum	Mama
music	Musik
Muslim	Moslem(in); muslimisch
my	mein(e)

make my bed – mein Bett machen

meet / **meeting** friends – Freunde treffen

N

name	Name; nennen
never	nie
new	neu
New Year	Neujahr
news	Nachrichten
nice	schön; nett
night	Nacht; Abend
no	nein; kein(e)
not	nicht
note	Notiz
now	nun, jetzt
number	Zahl, Nummer; nummerieren

Nice to meet you! –
   Schön, dich kennenzulernen!

take **notes** – Notizen machen

O

o'clock	Uhr
October	Oktober
odd one out	Wort, das nicht zu den anderen passt (bei Worträtseln)

It's three **o'clock**. – Es ist drei Uhr.

of	von	
often	oft	
old	alt	How **old** are you? – Wie alt bist du?
on	auf; an; in; am	
open	geöffnet	**on** Tuesday – dienstags
or	oder	**on** a tour – auf eine(r) Fahrt
orange juice	Orangensaft	
order	Reihenfolge	
other	andere(r, s)	
our	unsere(r, s)	
over	über; vorbei	
own	eigene(r, s)	your **own** – dein(e) eigene(r, s)

P

page	Seite	on **page** ... – auf Seite ...
pair	Paar	
palace	Palast	word **pair** – Wortpaar
parade	Umzug	
parents	Eltern	
part	Teil	sentence **part** – Satzteil
PE	Sportunterricht	
pencil	Bleistift	
penguin	Pinguin	
people	Leute, Menschen	
pet	Haustier	
phone	anrufen	
photo	Foto	
picnic	Picknick	
picture	Bild	
plant	Pflanze	
play	spielen	I **played** – ich spielte
player	Spieler(in)	**play** / **playing** football – Fußball spielen
playing	Spielen	
please	bitte	
poem	Gedicht	
polite	höflich	
postcard	Postkarte	
present	Geschenk; präsentieren	
programme	Programm, Sendung	TV **programme** – Fernsehsendung
pupil	Schüler(in)	
put	legen	
put on	anziehen	

Q

queen	Königin
question	Frage

R

rabbit	Kaninchen
rainy	regnerisch
read (out)	(vor)lesen
reading	Lesen
really	wirklich
rich	reich
right	rechts
room	Zimmer
rule	Regel
Russian	Russisch; russisch

Turn **right**. – Biege rechts ab.

S

sad	traurig
Saturday	Samstag
sausage	Würstchen
say	sagen
scene	Szene
school	Schule
science	Naturwissenschaft
Scotland	Schottland
season	Jahreszeit
second	zweite(r, s)
see	sehen; anschauen
sentence	Satz
she	sie
shoe	Schuh
shop	Geschäft, Laden
shopping	Einkaufen
sight	Sehenswürdigkeit
sign	Schild
sing	singen
singer	Sänger(in)
sister	Schwester
sit	sitzen
skirt	Rock
small	klein
snowy	verschneit
some	etwas; einige, ein paar
someone	jemand
soon	bald
Sorry!	Entschuldigung!
special	besondere(r, s)
sports	Sport-; Sportarten
sports centre	Sportcenter
spring	Frühling
station	Bahnhof, Station (z. B. U-Bahn)
Stop!	Stopp!

the **second** – der / die / das zweite

sentence part – Satzteil

go / going **shopping** – einkaufen gehen

I'm **sorry**. – Es tut mir leid.

story	Geschichte
straight on	geradeaus
street	Straße
strong	stark
subject	Fach
summer	Sommer
sun	Sonne
Sunday	Sonntag
sunny	sonnig
supermarket	Supermarkt
swimming	Schwimmen

go **swimming** – schwimmen gehen

T

take	nehmen, mitnehmen
teacher	Lehrer(in)
tell	erzählen
thanks / thank you	danke
that	der, die, das; dass
the	der, die, das
them	sie; ihnen
then	dann
there	dort; dorthin
there is / are ...	es gibt ..., da ist / sind ...
they	sie (Mehrzahl)
thing	Ding, Gegenstand
think	denken, glauben
third	dritte(r, s)
this	dies; diese(r, s)
Thursday	Donnerstag
tidy up	aufräumen
to	bis; zu; für; an; nach
today	heute
too	auch; zu
(the) top	ganz oben
tour	Rundfahrt, Tour
tower	Turm
trousers	Hose
true	wahr
Tuesday	Dienstag
Turkish	Türkisch; türkisch
turn	abbiegen
turn off	abschalten, ausschalten
TV	Fernseher

That's ... (= That is ...) – Das ist ...

the **third** – der / die / das dritte

I like tennis, **too**. – Ich mag auch Tennis.

from the **top** – von ganz oben

Turn left / right. – Biege links / rechts ab.

Turn off the music!

U

under	unter
understand	verstehen
us	uns
use	benutzen

V

Valentine's Day	Valentinstag
visit	besuchen

W

waiter / waitress	Kellner / Kellnerin
want	wollen
was	war
watch	anschauen, gucken; aufpassen
watching	Anschauen, Gucken
wax	Wachs
way	Weg
we	wir
wear	tragen
weather	Wetter
wedding	Hochzeit
week	Woche
weekend	Wochenende
welcome	willkommen
Get well!	Gute Besserung!
went	ging(en); fuhr(en)
what	was
What's ...? (= What is ...?)	Was ist ...?
when	wann; wenn; als
where	wo; woher
which	welche(r, s)
white	weiß
why	warum
will	werden
windy	windig
with	mit
woman	Frau
word	Wort
wordbank	Wortfeld
word pair	Wortpaar
word search	Wortsuchspiel
word web	Wortnetz
would	würde(st, en, et)

I **was** in London. – Ich war in London.

watch / **watching** TV – fernsehen, Fernsehen

What about you? – Was ist mit dir?
What did you do? –
  Was hast du gemacht?
What would you like to ...? –
  Was würdest du gern ...?

What's the English word for ...? –
  Was heißt ... auf Englisch?
What's on? – Was geht ab?

When do you get up? –
  Wann stehst du auf?

Where did you go on holiday? –
  Wo warst du in deinen Ferien?

Which ... do you like best? –
  Welche(n, s) ... magst du am liebsten?

Would you like ...? – Würdest du gern ...?

Y

year	Jahr
yes	ja
you	du; dich; dir; man
your	dein(e); euer / eure

... **years** old – ... Jahre alt

Z

zoo-keeper	Zoowärter(in), Tierpfleger(in)

The days of the week

Monday

Tuesday

Wednesday

Thursday

Friday

Saturday

Sunday

The months

January

February

March

April

May

June

July

August

September

October

November

December

The seasons

spring

summer

autumn

winter

Numbers

1	one
2	two
3	three
4	four
5	five
6	six
7	seven
8	eight
9	nine

9

10	**ten**
11	eleven
12	twelve
13	thirteen
14	fourteen
15	fifteen
16	sixteen
17	seventeen
18	eighteen
19	nineteen

20	**twenty**
21	twenty-one
22	twenty-two
23	twenty-three
24	twenty-four
25	twenty-five
26	twenty-six
27	twenty-seven
28	twenty-eight
29	twenty-nine

21

30	**thirty**
31	thirty-one
…	
40	**forty**
41	forty-one
…	
50	**fifty**
51	fifty-one
…	
60	**sixty**
61	sixty-one
…	
70	**seventy**
71	seventy-one
…	
80	**eighty**
81	eighty-one
…	
90	**ninety**
91	ninety-one
…	
100	**one hundred**

50

1 After the holidays

Holidays

1.	2	Back home
2.	3	Holiday activities (Karla)
3.	3	Holiday activities (George)

Back to school

4.	9	At school
5.	11	A new classmate
6.	12	In class

2 Around London

Famous sights

7.	1	Pictures
8.	2	New friends
9.	3	Some sights
10.	4	Sightseeing in London
11.	5	London sights
12.	7	How can I get there? (woman)
13.	7	How can I get there? (man)
14.	7	How can I get there? (child)
15.	8	Where is Rob?
16.	11	A London rap

London Zoo

17.	13	Zoo animals
18.	14	A tiger in London
19.	17	Lunch for the animals (penguins / gorillas)
20.	17	Lunch for the animals (hippos / tigers)
21.	17	Lunch for the animals (lions / zebras)
22.	18	Animals are …

3 Dreams

The future

23.	1	Charlie's future
24.	2	The future rap
25.	3	Dream jobs?
26.	4	Tell me the future!

Heroes

27.	7	Daydreams
28.	8	Robin Hood

4 Celebrations

Festivals

29.	1a)	Festivals
30.	1c)	Festivals
31.	2	A radio show (Karla)
32.	2	A radio show (Charlie)
33.	3	Let's celebrate
34.	4	At the Chinese New Year parade

Birthdays

| 35. | 13 | A special birthday |
| 36. | 14 | A birthday song |

5 Dos and don'ts

Rules at home

| 37. | 1 | Problems |
| 38. | 4 | Go to bed now! |

Rules at school

39.	8	Haverstock school rules
40.	14	What pupils say
41.	16	Let's be polite

6 Let's go!

What's on?

| 42. | 2 | Gillian and Karla |
| 43. | 5 | TV programmes |

Holidays

| 44. | 7 | Holidays in Britain |
| 45. | 9 | The dog in the fog |

Reading is fun

| 46. | A | The legend of Gelert |
| 47. | B | A horoscope |

Quellenverzeichnis

Audio-CD:

westermann GRUPPE

© 2016 Bildungshaus Schulbuchverlage Westermann Schroedel Diesterweg Schöningh Winklers GmbH Braunschweig, www.westermann.de

Listening texts are produced by John Green and recorded by Tim Woolf, London. Speakers: Fleur Ashton, Elise Bujega, Erin Clark, Melissa Collier, John Green, John Hasler, Layla Kahn, Harriet Kershaw, Kalucca Koniak, Rachael Miller, Paul Panting, Nigel Pilkington, Cameron Tweed, Maximus Woodward.

Songs:
16	A London rap. Recorded and arranged by Tim Woolf, London. Produced by John Green.
24	The future rap. Recorded and arranged by Tim Woolf, London. Produced by John Green.
36	A birthday song. Recorded and arranged by Tim Woolf, London. Produced by John Green.

Bildquellen:

|Alamy Stock Photo (RMB), Abingdon/Oxfordshire: 67photo 81.3; Adrian Sherratt 81.4; Arco Images / De Meester, J 54.1; BL Images Ltd 24.4; Bower, Jon 24.3; Caro 48.2; Chuck Pefley 6.1; Henn Photography / Cultura Creative 87.2; Hurst, D. 58.2; IanDagnall Laptop Computing 92.4; Image Source 83.2; Janine Wiedel Photolibrary/ Jacky Chapman 58.1; JGI/Jamie Grill / Blend Images 62.4; Jordan, Peter 27.4, 131.7; Kelly Redinger / Design Pics Inc. 83.1; Keuchel, Andreas 62.2; Michael Cullen 92.1; OJO Images Ltd 57.1, 62.3; Pegaz 58.3; Randy Duchaine 81.2; Steve Vidler 7.1, 19.2; SuperStock / Purestock 62.1; Turner, Bob 25.2; © Blend Images 62.5. |Avenue Images GmbH, Hamburg: FLPA/Malcolm Schuyl/ agefotostock 35.2; Index Stock/Ball, David 26.2, 131.3; Joe Fox/agefotostock 60.1. |Barker, Ruth, Plauen: 98.1. |bildagentur-online GmbH, Burgkunstadt: TIPS/Mitch Diamond 94.2. |Blickwinkel, Witten: Linke, R. 35.5; Sheldon, D. u. M. 35.6. |Bronwyn Grieve: 32.2. |Bulls Pressedienst GmbH, Frankfurt am Main: PRESSNET 92.5. |Caro Fotoagentur, Berlin: Sorge 8.2. |CartoonStock.com, Bath: 38.3, 38.4. |ddp images GmbH, Hamburg: Lennart Preiss 92.2. |dreamstime.com, Brentwood: 48.3; Dr_harry 35.10. |dsphotos.de / Dirk Schmidt Photography, Hamburg: Titel. |Eckart-Scheurig, Jutta, Wiesbaden: 24.1, 27.5. |Ehlers, Gisela, Hüttenwohld: 13.1, 85.1, 91.1, 91.2. |Fabian, Michael, Hannover: 15.1. |fotolia.com, New York: air 54.2; DeVIce 60.2; Jaspal Bahra 25.1, 131.5; Marina Zlochin 23.2; moonrun 6.2, 12.1, 19.3, 27.6, 38.2, 54.3, 60.3, 81.5, 91.4; Pawlowska, Edyta 48.1; Schwier, Christian 19.1; steffenw 23.1, 26.3, 131.4; taviphoto 35.1; © Anna Khomulo 90.1. |Getty Images, München: Damm/zefa 26.1; Francesco Ruggeri 48.6; Kitwood, Dan 38.1. |Hammersen-Schiffner, Bettina, Braunschweig: 27.2, 29.1, 32.1, 75.1, 131.8. |Interfoto, München: imagebroker/Schauhuber, Alfred 35.4; Neon 1 14.1; Travel Library / Grant Pritchard 58.4. |iStockphoto.com, Calgary: Chiang, Susan 98.2; Issaurinko 131.2; PeterBetts 35.8. |Klimczak, Emma, Hannover: 85.2. |mauritius images GmbH, Mittenwald: imagebroker 35.11; imagebroker/ Schulz, Ingo 35.7; Vidler 25.3. |Mohm, Julia, Braunschweig: 16.1, 16.2, 16.3. |OKAPIA KG - Michael Grzimek & Co., Frankfurt/M.: Radmila - Kerl/Mondberge.com 35.3; ZoomServerPro 35.12. |ONLY FRANCE.FR, Berlin: HENRI TABARANT 8.4. |PantherMedia GmbH (panthermedia.net), München: 81.1. |Picture-Alliance GmbH, Frankfurt a.M.: AP Photo 48.4; dpa 8.5; dpa/Karl-Josef Hildenbrand 58.5; dpa/R. Vennenbernd 24.2; dpa/Rousseau 27.1, 131.6; epa 27.3, 131.1; epa Geoff Caddick 24.5; epa Handout © dpa 92.3. |REUTERS, Berlin: Stephen Hird 91.3. |rsrdesign Gerlinde Reckels & Harry Schneider-Reckels, Wiesbaden: 90.2. |Shutterstock.com, New York: Ivanov, Anton 35.9; oneinchpunch 98.3. |stock.adobe. com, Dublin: CandyBox Images 98.5; ohishiftl 98.4. |Studio Schmidt-Lohmann, Gießen: 45.1, 48.5. |Tönnies, Frauke, Laatzen: 8.3. |transit - Fotografie und -Archiv, Leipzig: Hirth, Peter 8.1. |ullstein bild, Berlin: United Archives 92.6. |www. roggenthin.de, Nürnberg: 87.1, 94.1.

In class

Cut out the cards. Match the correct questions and answers.

Klebt die passenden Karten aneinander und locht sie oben. So bekommt ihr einen Fächer, mit dem ihr üben könnt.

× Where are you from?	I'm … years old.
× Have you got a pet?	Yes, I've got a …
× How old are you?	My hobby is …
× Where did you go on holiday?	My birthday is in …
× What's your name?	I'm from …
× When is your birthday?	My name is …
× What's your hobby?	I was in … / I was at home.

II A tiger game

🗣 **Play the game with your partner.**

Schneide den Tiger bei Aufgabe IV a) aus und lege ihn auf ein Foto. Dein Partner rät, wo er ist. Wechselt euch dann ab.

Buckingham Palace

the London Eye

Tower Bridge

London Zoo

Hyde Park

Madame Tussauds

Where is the tiger?
At Hyde Park?

No, it isn't.

At Tower Bridge?

Yes, it is.

Big Ben

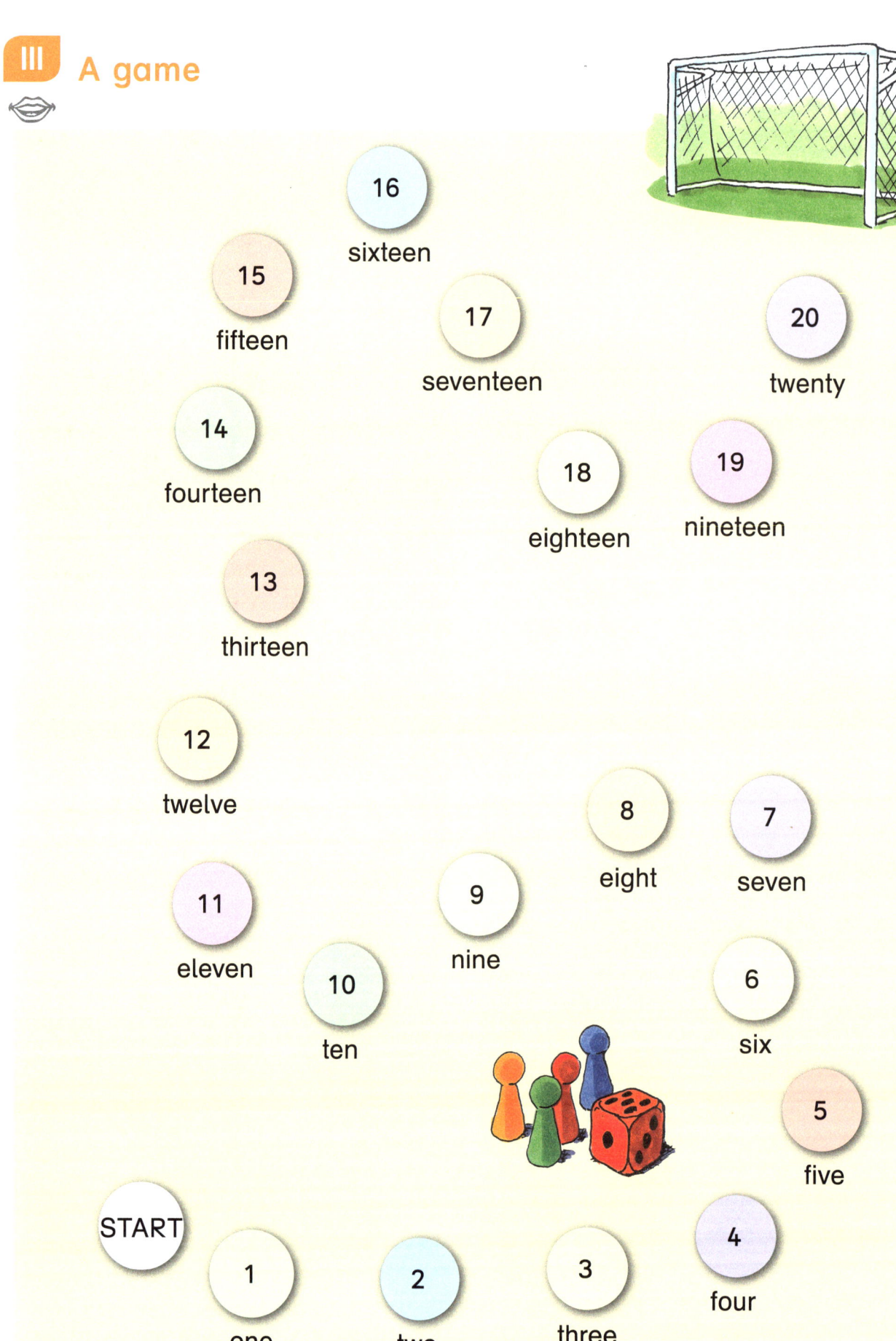

16 sixteen

15 fifteen

17 seventeen

20 twenty

14 fourteen

18 eighteen

19 nineteen

13 thirteen

12 twelve

8 eight

7 seven

11 eleven

9 nine

6 six

10 ten

5 five

START

1 one

2 two

3 three

4 four

IV a) Tell me the future!

Die Fragekarten zu diesem Spiel findest du bei Aufgabe IV b).
Schneide den Pfeil unten aus und befestige ihn in der Mitte des Kreises.

CAMDEN
MARKET
2

You will have a lot of friends.	You will have a sports car.
You will have eleven children.	You will have a big family.
You will be a pop star.	You will be a football player.
You will be a famous singer.	You will be a gardener.
You will live in New York.	You will live in a palace.
You will live in a big house.	You will live in Berlin.
You will have _____.	You will have _____.
You will be _____.	You will be _____.
You will live in _____.	You will live in _____.

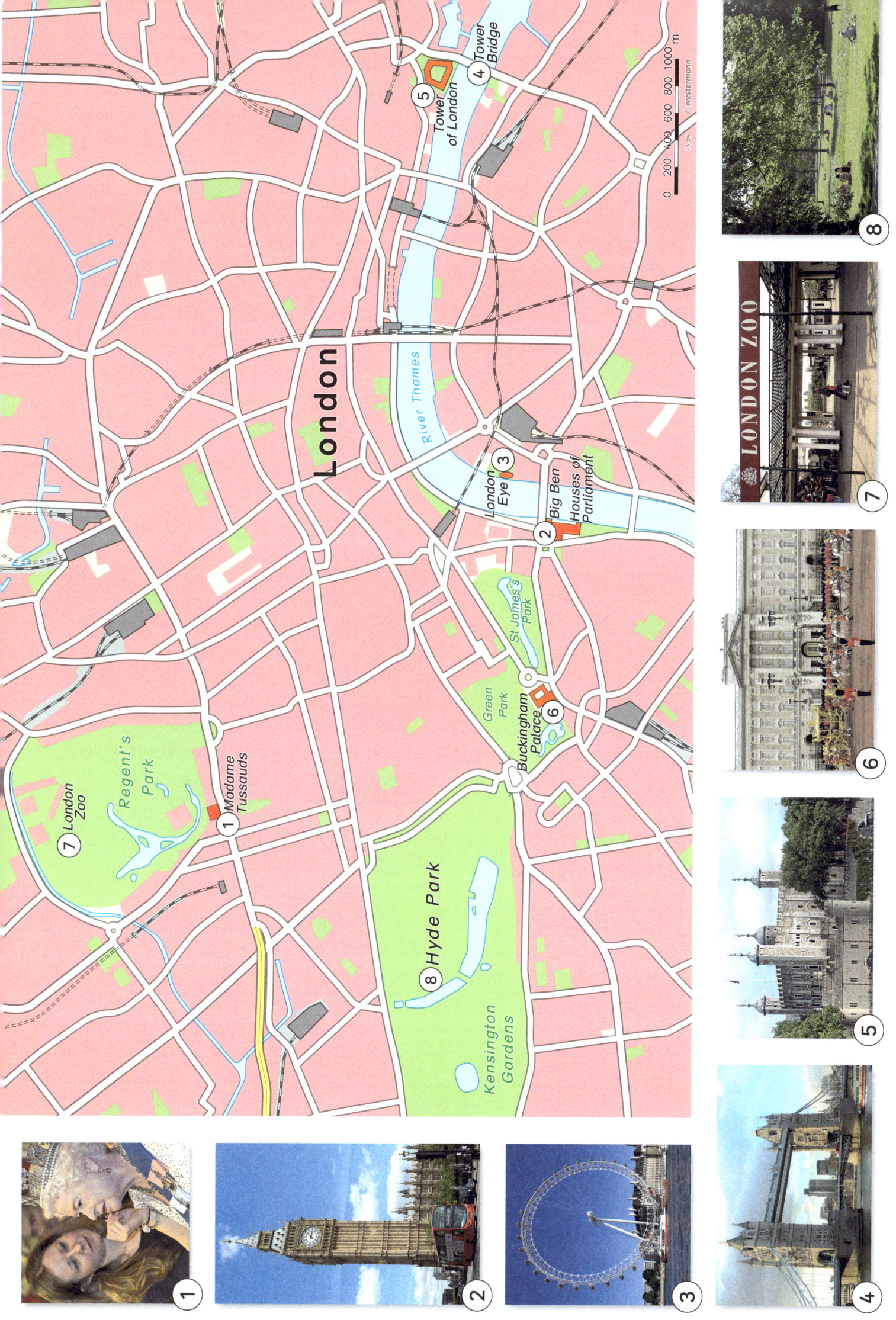

London

River Thames

1 Madame Tussauds

2 Big Ben / Houses of Parliament

3 London Eye

4 Tower Bridge

5 Tower of London

6 Buckingham Palace

7 London Zoo

8 Hyde Park

Regent's Park

Kensington Gardens

Green Park

St James's Park

0 200 400 600 800 1000 m

© Westermann

LONDON ZOO

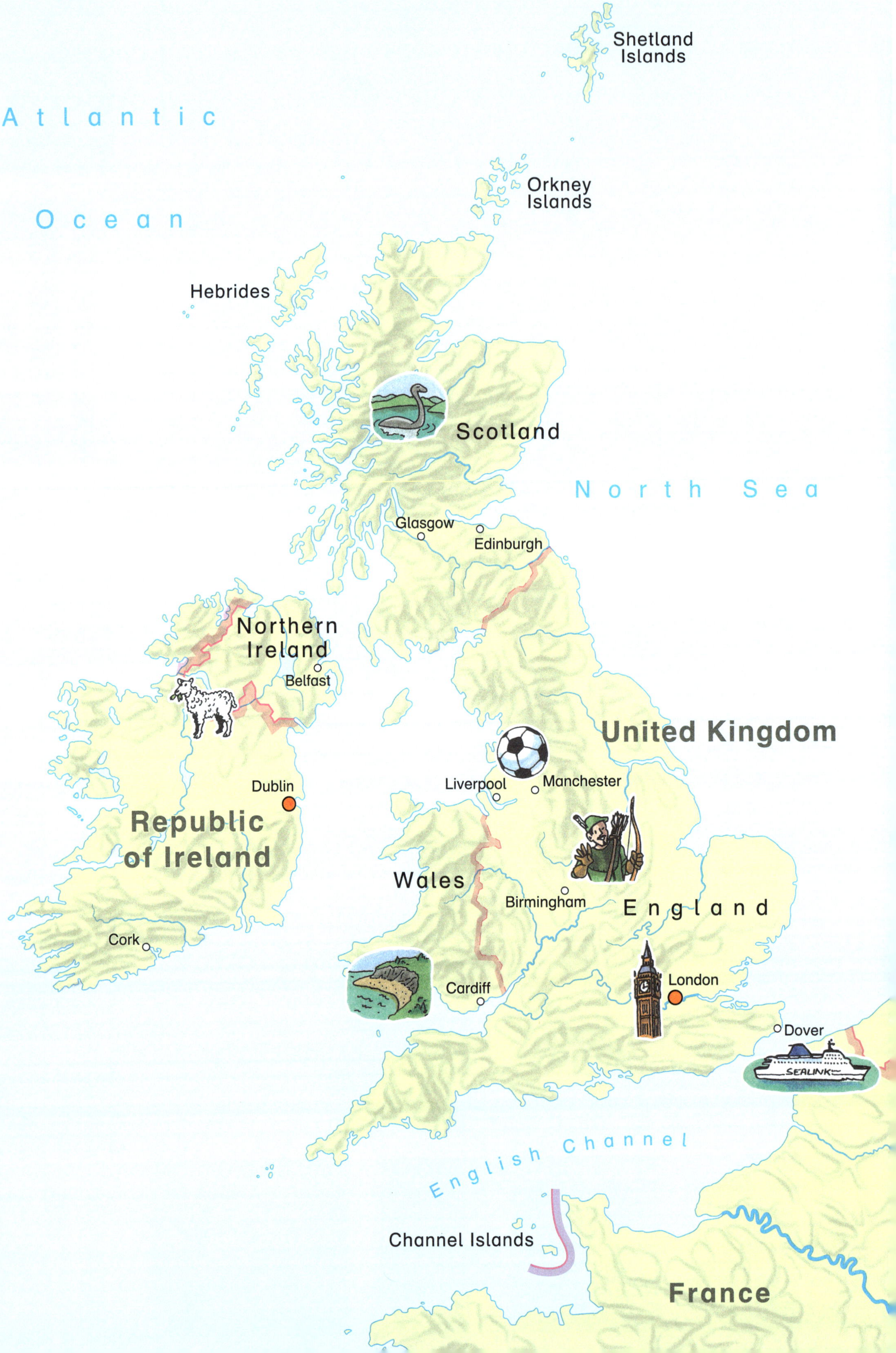

Atlantic

Ocean

Shetland
Islands

Orkney
Islands

Hebrides

Scotland

North Sea

Glasgow
Edinburgh

Northern
Ireland

Belfast

United Kingdom

Liverpool   Manchester

Republic
of Ireland

Dublin

Wales

Birmingham

England

Cork

Cardiff

London

Dover

English Channel

Channel Islands

France